The
Magnificent
Quest

Other works by Kelynda

The Crystal Tree:
A Structured Approach
to Reading Crystals and Colored Stones
(Whitford Press, 1987)

The Magnificent Quest

Practical Paths to the Inner Grail

Kelynda

A division of Schiffer Publishing, Ltd.
1469 Morstein Road
West Chester, Pennsylvania 19380 USA

The Magnificent Quest: Practical Paths to the Inner Grail
by Kelynda

Library of Congress Card Number: 90-61800
International Standard Book Number: 0-914918-87-7

Manufactured in the United States of America

Published by Whitford Press,
A division of
Schiffer Publishing Ltd.
1469 Morstein Road
West Chester, Pennsylvania 19380
Please write for a free catalog.
This book may be purchased from the publisher.
Please include $2.00 postage.
Try your bookstore first.

Contents

Acknowledgments   9

Part One: What Is the Inner Grail?   11

1. Defining the Inner Grail: An Introduction   13
The Quest 14 *The Grail and the Labyrinth: Two Myths* 15 *The Desert, the Monster, and Joy* 17 *Why Should You Go on the Quest?* 17

2. How to Use This Book   19
Designing the Journey 20 *What This Book Is* 21 *What This Book Is Not* 21 *Getting Started* 22 *While You Are Walking the Maze* 25 *Some Things to Expect* 26 *How Do You Begin?* 27

Part Two: Practical Paths   29

3. Smoke and Mirrors: Discovering Your Hidden Selves   31
The Essential Self 32 *The World and the Flesh* 41 *Memories* 48 *Spirit and Shadow* 53 *Notes* 64

4. The Power of Balance: Using the Four Elements   67
Four Spiritual Energies 68 *Fire* 69 *Earth* 69 *Air* 70 *Water* 70 *Finding Your Elements* 70 *Interpreting the Elements: Your Personality* 74 *Fire People* 74 *Earth People* 75 *Air People* 76 *Water People* 77 *Interpreting the Elements: The Elements and the Planets* 79 *Planets in Fire* 79 *Planets in Earth* 81 *Planets in Air* 83 *Planets in Water* 85 *Compatibility and the Elements: Some Principles* 87 *Fire Combinations* 90 *Earth*

Combinations 91 *Air Combinations* 92 *Water Combinations* 93 *Balancing the Elements* 94 *Notes* 97

5. Karma: Punishment or Preparation? 101
Karma as Punishment 101 *A New View of Karma* 103 *Discovering Your Karma* 105 *Notes* 109

6. Creativity and Renewal: Awakening Your Senses 115
Raising Awareness with Visualization 116 *Living in Harmony with the Earth* 127 *Exercises* 129

7. Divination: A Map Through the Maze 131
The Meaning and Uses of Divination 132 *Some Other Forms of Divination* 135 *The Fool* 137 *The Magician* 138 *The High Priestess* 139 *The Empress* 140 *The Emperor* 143 *The Hierophant* 144 *The Lovers* 145 *The Chariot* 146 *Justice* 147 *The Hermit* 148 *The Wheel of Fortune* 149 *Strength* 150 *The Hanged Man* 151 *Death* 152 *Temperance* 153 *The Devil* 154 *The Tower* 154 *The Star* 155 *The Moon* 155 *The Sun* 156 *Judgment* 157 *The World* 157 *Using the Tarot for Self-Discovery* 158 *Seeking Others' Counsel: How to Choose a Psychic* 162

8. The Wayfarer and the Citizen: Two Pathways to a Fulfilling Life 169
The Wayfarer 170 *The Citizen* 173 *Wayfarer or Citizen?* 175 *Note* 182

9. The Eyes of Heaven: Finding a Spiritual Perspective 185
Some Notes on Prayer 186 *The Quest for God* 191 *The Eyes of Heaven* 192 *Note* 193

10. Keys to Your Destiny 195
What Should I Do?: The Question of Destiny 196 *Determining Your Destiny: Exercises* 198 *Interpreting the Results* 204 *Living Well* 206 *Notes* 209

Further References 215

About the Author 219

for Bill, for always
and
in memory of my foremothers,
who wanted to write--

and did.

The important thing . . . is a force inside you, that belongs to you alone. It is yourself, actually, all that makes you a self. . . . Once you've found it, that force or will or need, whatever it is, then all you have to do is obey it--stay on the road it takes you.

--Ursula K. Le Guin, *Malafrena*

The questions which one asks oneself, begin, at last, to illuminate the world, and become one's key to the experiences of others.

--James Baldwin, *Nobody Knows My Name*

Men can starve from a lack of self-realization as much as they can from a lack of bread.

--Richard Wright, *Native Son*

Acknowledgments

Three groups of people were instrumental in helping me write this book: my husband, friends, and family, who offered affection and support during the arduous task of writing it; the writers, mystics, scientists, and psychologists--many of them long dead--whose ideas and theories provided an intellectual framework for my own quest and whose techniques I have borrowed and adapted; and my publishers, who physically produced the book.

Some people--my husband, in particular--helped in several ways. Bill asked me lots of challenging questions, and he never let me get away with facile answers. If that were all his contribution, I would still owe him an unpayable debt, but he did far more. His encouragement and praise were sweeter than anyone else's, and his deep faith in me made it unthinkable that I should quit--even when I wanted to. Not least, he nobly endured month after month of having his wife crawl out of bed in the middle of the night, spend hours writing in the next room, and creep back in again with icy feet.

Some friends have been with me throughout: Jean Kozul, Kathleen Brust, Janis Bucsko, Kathy Greenlaw, Elma Sabo, Courtney McCrae. My mother and sisters condoled with me on the days when writing was a chore and rejoiced with me when writing was a crown of glory. I thank Alexander Graham Bell for the telephone (but AT&T should thank *me*). Randy--the Reverend A. Rand Peabody--was my big brother, whose spiritual guidance calmed and challenged me, and whose careful, critical attention to my writing kept me at the top of my form.

Special thanks are owed to my dear friends at Staines; I wish them all long life, success, and happiness. Tony, Julian, George, and Charlotte were excellent company and a great refreshment when I tired of quests and labyrinths. Their friend, Albe, rapidly became my friend as well, and

I thank him for his stimulating conversation and wonderful letters. Tony showed me that courage and grace are twins, never happy when they're separated; her spirit is a white flame.

The kind and knowledgeable therapists who led me through my own mazes deserve thanks as well. Jackie Conrath enabled me to create a decent and pleasant life for myself, combining love and work. Jeanne Cervine helped me to set free my creativity and to trust myself and others. Jack Winegar guided me as I learned to accept my own success and stop crippling myself. All held up a true mirror to that terrified creature who scarcely dared to look; they helped me to know, love, and forgive myself and therefore to love others as well.

Those whose ideas have contributed to mine are too numerous to list here, but I thank everyone whose works are listed in the Further References. The poets, scientists, and novelists I quote may not deal directly with the how-tos of spiritual truth, but they are grappling with the same set of problems. I owe the late John Gardner special thanks, and for far more than the game of Smoke. His death--in a motorcycle accident on the road I grew up on--is an aching loss.

In the same vein, I cannot forget to thank those whose music played as I wrote, giving me energy and inspiration. *The Magnificent Quest* was chiefly fed by the extraordinary spiritual rock music of Steve Winwood, whose lyrics celebrate the blessings of both night and morning and whose music sets fingers dancing on the computer keyboard--even in the icy light of a December dawn. I also owe credit to Pink Floyd (especially for their stirring "On the Turning Away"), Steeleye Span, Bruce Hornsby and the Range, the Alan Parsons Project, and Eric Clapton (for "Layla"). Without their music, and that of Beethoven, Bach, and the Beatles, there would be no book.

As you read, remember that I, too, am working all these things out for myself; I have not (by any stretch of the imagination) solved all my problems, dealt with all my fears and scars, and learned to live always on the highest plane. Like you, I am still struggling. As I write, I pray for you, my readers; I pray that my words will help you find enlightenment and not be a stumbling block to you. As you work through the exercises and ponder my ideas, pray for me as well.

Finally, you, dear readers, deserve my thanks. Let me know how your quests turn out.

Kelynda

Part One:

What Is the Inner Grail?

Chapter 1

Defining the Inner Grail: An Introduction

Ask, and it shall be given you; seek, and ye shall find; knock, and it shall be opened unto you.
                                        --Matthew 7:7

Here begins the new life.
  --Dante, *La Vita Nuova*

I give you the end of a golden string
  Only wind it into a ball.
It will lead you in at heaven's gate
  Built in Jerusalem's wall.
        --William Blake, "Jerusalem"

What is the inner grail? Why should you seek it?

Like the light, the grail itself is hard to define and impossible to hold in your hand. It is not a prize found once or won in a lottery and then kept forever. It is not a golden trophy to put on your mantelshelf and dust once a week. It is not a verbal or mathematical formula that can be memorized and recited by rote. You cannot deposit it in a bank or list it on your resume.

The inner grail balances your life and the Universe. It fulfills your individuality by showing where you fit in the shimmering dance of a meaningful, created Universe. It illumines your karma, showing how your personality and the events of your life fit into a pattern, and it sets forth your destiny, showing what you are meant to do with your unique talents and experience. It can help you make sense of your history and discover your place in the Universe. It can help you find joy in daily life and meaning in your work. It can help you discover what you truly value, and thereby simplify your life. It can help you understand your past and forgive yourself and others. It can teach you to tap into your own reservoirs of power, creativity, and imagination and enable you to understand the great myths of the world.

The inner grail changes you and your way of acting, reacting, seeing, feeling, living. You can call it joy, or inner peace, or enlightenment, or balance, or a sense of where you are, but all these definitions are inadequate. The phrase "the spiritual life" may come closest, but it can evoke an image of pale ascetics starving in the desert instead of a whole world glowing, illumined, on fire with spirit and meaning and joy. Perhaps there is our definition: The inner grail can be seen only by what it illumines, and it illumines daily life, giving you a glimpse of the kingdom of heaven within you.

THE QUEST

Finding the inner grail is a quest, a process of self-discovery. On the quest, you will perform three tasks: finding and fulfilling your destiny, dealing with karma, and learning to live well. This book offers questions, not answers--questions you must ask yourself. You have a destiny, a mission. What is it? There are interlocking levels of life. How can you live deeply and righteously on all of them?

You will answer those questions by looking within yourself. The questions and exercises will help you keep a balanced outlook, so that you explore all the provinces of the grail country. Written journals and exercises will help you keep track of where you have been and how you have grown.

The essential process is this: You must allow yourself to see the truth; it has always been there, and you have always known it, but you may never have faced and accepted it. You start by looking at it, which does not mean simply acknowledging its existence and turning away; you must let yourself feel it. Then you tell it--whatever it is--in a metaphor, a dance, a journal, a prayer. Until you can tell it truthfully, you will never be free. Then, in the telling, the truth becomes transformed, and so do you. The truth becomes art and you become capable of seeing it, not only from your own perspective, but with new spiritual eyes. This is the only magical part of the process; it cannot be explained, but it can be experienced. In seeing and telling the truth, you will find freedom.

The search begins with the quest for your karma, for the meaning of who you are and what has happened to you. Once you have found and understood the essential pattern of your life, you can go on to the quest for your destiny. When you know who you are, you will be able to understand what you must do.

Best of all, the search is guided. This book will help you ask yourself questions, help you find the patterns in the answers, help you put the patterns together into your unique road map. You must take the journey, but the book offers practical guides to every step on the way.

Achieving the inner grail is worth crossing deserts, worth threading mazes and facing monsters. Once you taste it, you will thirst for it forever. You can find it *if* you are willing to go on the quest, *if* you are willing to explore the labyrinth.

THE GRAIL AND THE LABYRINTH: TWO MYTHS

A multitude of myths and symbols express the truth of the quest. (Do not mistake the shadow for the substance; the truth is far beyond and above anything I can write about it. Myths come closest to expressing the truth, but even they use indirection and metaphor. The shining reality of the truth is far greater.) Among these are the stories of the grail quest and of the labyrinth. Both myths show how self-discovery leads to freedom. Through self-knowledge (the question answered, the maze explored) you can find release.

Myths, it should be explained, are not lies, fallacies, or the simpleminded attempts of primitive people to explain natural phenomena, no matter what you were taught in school. That condescending attitude has begun to give way to an understanding of their true role and significance. Myths are some of the finest and deepest expressions of essential human situations that have ever been created. They are precious maps to the unconscious mind and to the spiritual world--as are fairy tales and many novels, songs, and poems. Few sloppy uses of language are as deceptive and destructive as the careless use of myth for *fallacy* or *untruth*. (See the list of references for some of the great works on the meaning of myths.)

Briefly, here are the two myths that so perfectly express our quest.

> In a bleak and waterless land a fool is travelling. Not just travelling; the fool (sometimes called Parsival) is on a quest: the hunt for the Grail. The fool asks directions of a fisherman, who is casting his line into the polluted and dwindled waters of this country in drought. The directions lead the fool to the Grail castle. There again the fisherman appears: He is the king of this country, and he is sick with an old wound. With a word, a question, the fool heals him. Because the king and the country are one, the drought ends; the waters are freed. They return to the land, which blooms again in exuberant and joyous fertility.

> A man (Theseus) and a woman (Ariadne) are standing in the dark. She has led him through the maze, through the twisted, night-haunted corridors of the labyrinth. He has come to slay the monster (his half-brother) that, every year, demands and devours the finest youth of the country. The sacrifice has become intolerable. The hero will end it. And then? Joy. Freedom. The end of fear and the beginning of a new life.

Perhaps the stories (greatly abbreviated here) are strange to you. What do they mean?

The grail quest is the search for a meaning to life. You and I and all who have ever hunted for something they could neither name nor see are fools, as Parsival was, because we do not know where we are going even though we are rushing to get there as fast as we can. The treeless land we wander is our own bleak and blasted life; the fisher-king, healed with the right question, is ourselves.

The hero's exploration of the labyrinth is the search for destiny. Having gone through the maze--begun to understand yourself--you must become a hero and slay the monster. This book is like Ariadne, guiding you through the maze and out again so that you no longer need to sacrifice your talents, ambitions, and dreams to the monster in the dark of the labyrinth.

No one else can free you, but you can free yourself. Whether your quest is for creativity, peace, love, or fulfillment, the essential process is the same. This book is a guidebook to the grail country, telling you who and what you are likely to meet on the road to the castle. It is--to change the metaphor--a road map through the labyrinth; at the center is some-thing (blood kin to us) that must be faced and conquered. After the grail is found and the monster slain, there is joy.

THE DESERT, THE MONSTER, AND JOY

The grail story begins with suffering and despair in a desert land. The labyrinth is dark and dirty, and in the middle waits a monster you must kill. On the face of it, both ways of telling the quest story may seem uninviting: who wants to begin a quest that entails dealing with loneli-ness or fear or pain?

The answer is: *Those who are looking for joy.* Trouble comes whether you believe in it or not; it's better to know how to deal with it before it happens. Some people spend their whole lives denying that anything painful can happen. In their desperate disavowals of suffering I see an intolerable fear, and I pity them. Someday they will come face to face with a trouble that cannot be denied, and they will have no words to speak to that trouble, no assurance that they can survive it, no way to discover the meaning of it, no road to come to joy afterward. Indeed, they are usually so eager to stave off pain that they are equally unable to experience joy.

But if you are brave enough to look pain in the face, you can hear its message and learn. You can change yourself. You can find joy in little pleasures even when the rest of your life is a shambles. You will know that, having already survived pain, you can survive it again.

This book is about joy: true joy, not the synthetic product of ignor-ing or devaluing our true feelings but the joy that comes from a life lived richly. It is about how to find it in yourself and spread it through your life. You may have to cross some deserts and thread some labyrinths to find it. The deserts and the dark walls are there for a purpose, though, and by the time you play all the games and write down your thoughts and do all the meditation exercises, you will find that purpose and under-stand the unique shape of your journey.

WHY SHOULD YOU GO ON THE QUEST?

Why bother? Why cross deserts and thread mazes? Because it is a full, complete way to live. Because it works. Because you're going to be living anyway, and it is better to find the meaning and purpose of your life than to waste it. Because now is the only time you have to live. The process is as important as the goal. The quest is a way to live, not just a procedure.

The life of the quest is that what we are designed for. Humans can never be entirely fulfilled by a purely materialistic life. You need something to help you find the meaning in your life--not, notice, to give your life meaning. It *has* meaning now; you just may not have found it yet.

The inner grail will not simply come to you; you must go and look for it. Though joy is important, joy is not the inner grail; it is merely one thing--and by no means the only thing--that may come with the quest. It is not mere self-knowledge or self-understanding or even self-acceptance, though all three contribute to it.

It is not a mere selfish and individual illumination. The grail teaches you to love your neighbor as yourself, to understand and to forgive, to appreciate the glorious intricacies of the created Universe and of lilacs in the spring rain. To the finder of the grail, the Earth is alive and joyous; the Universe dances; all individuals have value, uniqueness, glory. The grail makes room for love: love for the starving and homeless, for the friend and neighbor, for the Earth herself. It is ever-changing and growing, a living light.

But can we reach that unalterable peace? The process of questing is as far as most of us will ever come to attaining the grail itself. We may get better at the quest, but we will not reach the culmination until the hour of our deaths, perhaps not even then. Yet the search itself is so rewarding, so exquisite, that I may be forgiven for using the words "grail" and "quest" almost interchangeably. Western society is so achievement-oriented that we tend to forget that the process of doing, of becoming, is as important as the final product. Choosing to go on the quest, asking the serious questions, making a commitment to God and the truth--these are the beginnings of the new life.

Chapter 2

How to Use This Book

Ye shall know the truth, and the truth shall set you free.
--John 8:32

Peace...can only be achieved by understanding.
--Albert Einstein, *Notes on Pacifism*

Truth is not only the fulfillment of our own being; it is that by which things outside of us have an existence.

The fulfillment of our being is moral sense. The fulfillment of the nature of things outside ourselves is intellect.

These, moral sense and intellect, are the powers or faculties of our being. They combine the inner or subjective and the outer or objective use of the power of the mind. Therefore, with truth, everything done is right.

--Confucius, *Analects*

No one can hand you the truth. You have to find it yourself. Thus, this book does not list the truths--about yourself, about the world, about God--that you will begin to understand when you have found your own inner grail. *The Magnificent Quest* is designed to let you discover the truth for yourself. Only then will you believe it, because only then will it be your own.

When you are seeking the grail, the journey itself is part of the process of growth and healing. But precisely how do you quest? What makes living the questing life any different from just living your life haphazardly? Most of us do not have a clear idea of how to go forth (or inward), seeking truth. How should you prepare for the journey? Where do you go first? What kind of adventures can you expect? This chapter will clarify these issues and give you some--not all--of the answers. Some answers you will have to find for yourself.

DESIGNING THE JOURNEY

The inner grail is a balance between yourself and the Universe, based on--but not limited to--knowledge of yourself and awareness of the magnificence of creation. It is worth seeking, but it must be sought. No one can hand it to you in a neat package or inject you with the magic solution of enlightenment. You can be guided but not dragged along the path to the grail. Ultimately, the questions asked and the answers given must be your own. You yourself have to work it through, fight it out, learn its lessons, and make it your own. Individual experience counts for everything.

This truth accounts for the design of this book. I have provided essays, exercises, and quotations from other writers and thinkers. The essays may help you clarify your feelings, stimulate your thoughts, suggest new paths to search, offer useful distinctions and categories, provide some valuable information, or inspire some new dreams in you-- even, perhaps, incite controversy. The exercises are designed to help you discover what you think and feel and to provide a (mostly written) record of your process of questing. They will help you find your destiny; discover the pattern of your karma; and get to know the parts of yourself that have been suppressed, repressed, oppressed, and forgotten. You will find quotations from great minds on each chapter title page that express some varied viewpoints on the chapter's contents. I hope you will go beyond the quotations, back to the original works to see what great minds have made of the problems you are facing. For the eager, the curious, or the scholarly, there is a list of further references.

The design of this quest presupposes two essential truths: that there is meaning and purpose in your life, a meaning and purpose that are at least partly discoverable and that you should try to discover; and that good and evil exist. If you choose to explore the "pleasures" of evil in this lifetime, you will pay. Your acts and attitudes have consequences; what you do matters.

What if I am wrong, and there is no afterlife at all? Then the way of life I have outlined here will still have given you satisfaction, meaning, and joy. You will have discovered richness and beauty in ordinary things and you will have helped other people as well as yourself.

Some Special Terms

I use the term *karma* in a special way. Leaving aside the question of the contribution of previous lives, I define karma as the specific set of situations and problems that you're in this life to deal with. If your destiny is to champion the oppressed, your karma will probably place you in some painful situations in order to sensitize you to the effects of oppression.

Destiny, like karma, has a special meaning in this book. It is not a fatalistic, predetermined doom that you cannot avert. Indeed, you have a choice whether or not to fulfill your destiny. It is the purpose you were created for--and it isn't always glamorous.

WHAT THIS BOOK IS

This book is a workbook for helping you identify, search for, and (I hope) find your own inner grail. It is filled with questions, exercises, and suggestions that may help you learn to live creatively and with joy, identify your karma, and fulfill your destiny. The exercises can help you discover and express your own inner treasures and learn to live in a healthy, creative, and satisfying way. As a tool for self-discovery, *The Magnificent Quest* may help you enrich your life, find joy in love and work, learn to love your neighbor as yourself, and identify what you want from life.

I have tried to be fair and unbiased, but, inevitably, *The Magnificent Quest* was shaped by my experiences, beliefs, and spiritual traditions as well as by extensive reading, thinking, prayer, research, and discussions with people whose experiences and beliefs have taken them on different paths or whose view of our shared beliefs is radically different from mine. You, too, may disagree with me fundamentally and unalterably. Nevertheless, the techniques offered here can help you find your own path to the grail.

WHAT THIS BOOK IS NOT

The Magnificent Quest is designed to help you find your own path of self-discovery. It is not a definitive statement of the Truth, and I don't claim to be the sole dispenser of wisdom, a paragon of perfection, or any kind of messiah. The book's value is enhanced by the fact that it is intended for--and written by--the ordinary, struggling human being, not the super-guru who has never suffered, struggled, doubted, or cried. Because I have lived through disasters (some of them unusual, some of them ordinary, all of them both painful and educational), I can offer assurance to you: You will get through. There is a meaning to life. You can discover that meaning for yourself. This is one way to start looking.

The Magnificent Quest is a highly individual guide to self-knowledge. *In no sense is it a substitute for* medical, psychological, or psychiatric treatment. These things have their place in life; you have to judge when and whether you need them. No spiritual exercises from a book can cure mental or physical illness or heal deep emotional scars. If you have been raped, abused, or traumatized; if you are depressed, manic, or having hallucinations; if, in any other way, you have serious problems, *seek counseling*. It is no shame and no disgrace; it can help you deal with the past, function in the present, and plan a good future. I know because I have benefited immeasurably from it, and I will probably return to it later. Like vitamins and minerals, it's good for you. This book, helpful as it may be to leading a balanced and dynamic life, is no substitute for professional treatment.

GETTING STARTED

At last we leave the realm of theory and get down to practicalities: what you will need to use this book, how you should prepare, and what to expect along the way.

Necessary Equipment

The first thing you'll need is a notebook and a good pen or pencil. Don't skimp on these. Ask yourself what size, shape, color, and quality of paper you like, and get it. A leather portfolio is no better than a legal pad, provided that the legal pad makes you more comfortable. The standard of taste and usefulness is your own experience. Indeed, selecting a notebook is your first exercise in discovering what you really like and desire. (If you prefer loose paper, you'll need a file or something to keep your notes together.)

As for pens, use the same standards. If you prefer to use a mechanical pencil or a fountain pen, get it and use it; if you like felt-tip pens, use them. Choose a color of ink or a softness of lead that makes it easy for you to write. The act of writing should be a physical pleasure.

If, like me, you are hooked on writing on a computer, try to be as comfortable as possible when working on it. You should also get a notebook and pen for those times when a computer is out of your reach.

As well as writing paper, you'll need an artist's sketchbook or some kind of paper to draw on. I like a soft lead pencil and a rather toothy, textured paper to draw on. What do you like? Perhaps you want to use crayons, pastels, watercolors, tempera, or other media for the "drawing" exercises. Use what you like best. Moreover, there's no need to stick with a single medium. You may feel that some drawings are more expressive when made with pen and ink, while others demand the bright unblended colors of crayons. Don't worry if you are a poor artist. This is not going to be an art competition, and you won't be expected to draw like da Vinci. I can't draw like Dali, much less da Vinci.

Essential equipment also includes absolute privacy for your journals and notebooks. You don't want to even begin to be afraid that someone has found your private writings. A locked and hidden box can prevent your children and/or your parents from reading things that don't concern them. If you live alone or with a trustworthy partner, you may not need to take this precaution. Still, you'll need solitude, space, and peace to do the exercises. Try to schedule time alone for grail-questing. It is just as important--no, more important--than time at the gym.

Optional Equipment

Some exercises are done with crystals and Tarot. You can work through the book without a set of stones and a Tarot deck, but you may want to consider buying them. If money is a factor, the most important is the Tarot deck.

If you're inexperienced with the cards, choosing from among the hundreds of available decks can be a daunting task. Approach it as you did the notebook. Which one do you like? Try to find a store that has open decks for your examination, but *never* buy an open deck. You want the cards to carry your own vibrations, not those of all the passing strangers who handled it before you did. Get a regular Tarot deck; some fortune-telling cards are based on other systems. Though they may be useful, they're unlikely to have the major arcana, on which much of *The Magnificent Quest* is based. I would also not recommend the Crowley/

Thoth deck, which is based on his peculiar ideas. In his deck Strength is renamed Lust, for example. However, if these cards speak most strongly to you, feel free to use them.

If you are an experienced reader, you may consider getting a deck that you don't already use for readings. A slight change of symbolism or even of artistic style can give you new and unexpected insights into the familiar world of the Tarot.

The crystal set used in *The Magnificent Quest* is based on the eighteen crystals of *The Crystal Tree*. You don't need to have the book to do these exercises, but you do need a range of stones, colored and clear, opaque and crystalline. If you don't have a good balance of stones, your results will be skewed. You need the full range of options or you will limit the effectiveness of your choice.

To choose crystals, lay the crystals in a shallow dish (wood is nice but not necessary) or in a cloth bag large enough for your hand. Close your eyes and let your fingers and hands choose. They will sense your vibrations.

Other divinatory tools--runes, the I Ching, Star+Gate, books on numerology and palmistry and all the other psychic disciplines--can come later.

As nearly essential as the Tarot is an accurate horoscope chart. It is far beyond the scope of this book to teach you to interpret your own chart, much less anyone else's, but it will help when you're working with the four elements. If you have no money and/or no exact birth time, find an astrological ephemeris and photocopy the page where your date of birth appears. Though you won't have your rising sign, you'll at least have an idea of where your other planets are. It is not ideal, but it will do.

Other useful (but not necessary) equipment is music to dance to, a tape recorder to tape spoken or sung exercises, an exercise mat, comfortable clothes (comfortable nudity is perfectly acceptable if your neighbors or housemates don't mind), a deep bathtub with plenty of hot water, a stock of herbal teas and a pretty teacup, good walking and dancing shoes, and a circle of friends to share some exercises with.

A Few Notes on Technique

Throughout the book, notes on technique appear. Different sets of exercises emphasize different techniques that appeal to different powers and parts of the brain. Though one technique may seem to work best for you, I urge you to try all the techniques; you owe it to yourself to develop your hidden skills.

Writing exercises call on a synthesis of right-brain imagination and left-brain analysis. You are not writing for school here, so don't worry about grammar, syntax, or spelling. Write what you feel and think. You will find that ideas come when you are not forcing them. Unless you're already comfortable with the process of writing, it's best to take a few minutes to think about the exercise before you get out your notebook. When you have several ideas, start writing.

Music and art exercises help you explore feelings and tastes. All the arts help us express feelings that we might not otherwise be able to reach and sense. Through the exercises here, you can discover your hidden emotions, sometimes by doing art, drawing or singing or dancing your feelings; sometimes by experiencing art, listening to music that helps you feel.

Dance, massage, and other physical exercises help you listen to your body. Visualization exercises help you test your choices before you commit yourself to them and help you remember things you have forgotten. The metaphor games can be played alone or with groups of dear friends.

WHILE YOU ARE WALKING THE MAZE

Every day, as long as you are actively on the quest, you should do three things. It doesn't matter if you plan to do any exercises that day or not; until you've finished the labyrinth or given up, you're on the quest.

Write your dreams in your notebook. If you want to analyze them, feel free; if not, just record them. Ideally, you'll write down the dreams as well as your feelings about the day to give yourself a complete picture. Do not worry if you can't make any sense out of them yet.

Spend some time in silent meditation or prayer. This is as vital as recording your dreams. You're going to be putting forth a great deal of spiritual effort and energy; this restorative time is absolutely essential. Start your day with at least five minutes, and give yourself five minutes or more at the close of the day as well. All day long, seize whatever moments you can for silent communion with God. Besides the spiritual benefits, you'll find yourself with more energy, more patience, and probably also lower blood pressure. Don't forget praise as an important element of prayer! A spontaneous thank-you--for the weather, the scenery, the chance to live, even for trials and tribulations--can be extraordinarily uplifting. (See Chapter 9 on prayer and divination for some thoughts on the process and meaning of prayer.)

Do something purely physical. The process of *centering down* (a Quaker term for preparing to meditate) can work physically as well. Become aware of the skin encasing you, your barrier from and connection to the world outside. Sense the bones--sturdy, uncompromising--that shape and structure you. Feel the blood surging and ebbing in veins and arteries, whole, circular, cleansing, nourishing. Sense the electricity of your nerves and brain. Relax. Feel your soft, moist, sensitive tongue. Listen to your body. You can do this lying down in a quiet spot, walking outdoors, or in the shower or bath. It helps to do it the same way daily for a few days, perhaps a week, then change to a new way. However you choose to begin listening to your own body's wisdom, keep at it.

SOME THINGS TO EXPECT

Questing isn't always a picnic. Sometimes there is a rush of joy as you make new discoveries, change your life, and stretch your wings. Sometimes there is a flood of pain as you explore old wounds. When you change old attitudes and learn new ones, the entrenched ways of doing and seeing fight back. It is a struggle. Enlightenment is not easily found, though once you've tasted it, you know that they speak the truth when they say it is your natural condition, what you've been yearning for. If the reaction becomes too strong, once again, consider professional help.

Because you'll be recording your dreams daily, you may experience a sudden upswing in the number, vividness, and perhaps strangeness of your dreams. This is normal even though the dreams may be frightening. What has happened is that you've begun to pay attention to your unconscious mind, which communicates as directly as it can through dreams. You may be confronted with a backlog of dream material, issues that you have been unconsciously working through. Write them all down.

The new awareness of your body can manifest itself as joy or pain, depending on your physical experiences to date. You may change the way you eat, begin to exercise more, and experience new sexual feelings. Old habits may slip away or you may fight to hold on to certain physical comforts that you now see are self-destructive--smoking, for example. Let the changes happen as slowly as they need to. When you are ready to change, change will begin to come.

HOW DO YOU BEGIN?

You begin by beginning. Make sure you have enough time--an hour or more--to start with. Don't forget your pen and notebook. Don't edit your answers. Honesty is paramount. Don't try too much at once.

Because ritual is important, you may want to start your work on the book the same way each time. Use relaxation exercises--breathing and tea-drinking, yoga, or whatever works for you. Pray for peace and enlightenment, for wisdom and grace, and for guidance on the long journey.

Ask. Seek. Knock.

Begin.

Part Two:

Practical Paths

Chapter 3

Smoke and Mirrors: Discovering Your Hidden Selves

The humble knowledge of thyself is a surer way to God than
the deepest search of science.
> --Thomas à Kempis, *The Imitation of Christ*

Resolve to find thyself, and know that he
Who finds himself, loses his misery.
> --Matthew Arnold, "Self-Dependence"

The kingdom of God is within you.
> --Luke 17:21

Self-knowledge is the essential clue that will help you thread the maze of your karma and your destiny. Though it sounds easy to know yourself--who else can you know, if not yourself?--it is far more complex than it seems. There are two reasons. One is that, in general, we experience ourselves from the inside out; everything is subjective and may be distorted. We see the motives and reasons for any action, while others see only the action. Moreover, we may not be aware of what we are doing and its effect on others. The second reason is that the true self is elusive, hiding conventions, assumptions, and expectations. The self's first imperative is to preserve itself; it is willing to assume a disguise in order to gain acceptance and therefore safety.

Think of the self as a unicorn--immortal, separate, immaculate. Traditionally, the unicorn could not be approached except by a virgin. (The virgin was less a symbol of physical than of spiritual purity.) Unicorn hunts were not a grim affair of stalking through the snow, wearing camouflage pants and fluorescent-orange caps; they were lively processions, designed to attract the unicorn with music, dancing, and beauty. You cannot drag the self out with Gestapo tactics; only a loving (and indirect) approach will capture the unicorn of your soul.

You don't need processions of white-robed girls and chiming bells to lure your inner unicorn into the light. Games, yes; subtle strategies, of course. This chapter is called "Smoke and Mirrors"--a traditional description of both sleight-of-hand and politics--because the quest for the self partakes in certain ways of both things. In magic there are deceptions, ploys, distractions; if you can see beyond them you may see the truth. In politics image is everything; the hidden self acts like a politician running for office, saying whatever the constituent wants to hear, in order to stay popular, powerful, alive. Smoke is also a metaphor game; mirrors are also ways of looking into the inner self.

The exercises in this chapter can help you begin to understand your essential self--the self you were born to be, the self that has been guided and shaped by experiences good and bad. By looking in the mirrors of metaphor and visualization, you will begin the process of self-discovery, but you will not finish it. It never ends.

This chapter is a good beginning place. It is arranged in four sections: the Essential Self, the World and the Flesh, Memories, and Spirit and Shadow. You will find that the four sections roughly correspond to the four elements: the essential self is like fire, the world and the flesh like earth, memories like air, and the spirit like water. (More information on the four elements is given in Chapter 4.) Each area of your life demands a slightly different approach. Though some exercises are similar--all areas use journal entries, for example--each area demands unique exercises. Metaphors are an ideal tool when you seek the essential self, for example, but dancing and crafts are more helpful when you are trying to reconcile yourself with the world and the flesh.

THE ESSENTIAL SELF

A hunt for the essential self is something like trying to capture a ray of sunlight. Though you can see things--including motes of dust and sometimes the air itself--*by the* light, *you can never see the light itself.* (This explains why outer space is dark; though plenty of light travels through it, there is nothing there to be seen, so the light simply passes through, not itself visible without something real and concrete to catch it.) Light lives by its function of illumination, as the essential self lives by its expression through work, play, desires, tastes. You know it's there, because you can see and feel its effects, but you cannot catch or tame it.

How then can we find the essential self? We can look only for its tracks, and one of the simplest and most accurate ways to track the self is by metaphor. Metaphor is a term from literature, meaning a figure of speech that compares an object to something else, either directly ("My husband is an angel") or indirectly, as a simile ("She cooks like an angel"). The best metaphors express the truth in ways that no literal words can. They give an instantaneous grasp of the subject. When I say that my husband is an angel (a hackneyed metaphor that happens to be accurate), you can instantly, without meeting him, know that he has the qualities of an angel: kindness, sweetness of disposition, and spiritual strength.

Metaphors can help you discover the truth about your essential self. Indeed, the first exercise, the game "Smoke," is pure metaphor. Smoke asks you to imagine what you would be if you were not a person but were still yourself. If you were a tree, a landscape, a musical instrument, a machine, what would you be? Perhaps you would be an oak; steep, wooded, unglaciated slate hills runnelled with streams; a full-bellied lute; a movie projector. Or maybe you would be a sweet-blooded maple or a flowering cherry; a rising escarpment or the Painted Desert; a magnificent pipe-organ or a lonesome harmonica; a sporty small car or a Cray supercomputer.

By throwing off (at least in imagination) the outward signs of being a human, you can come close to an image of your true self. This is not a popularity contest; you are not being asked to tell your favorite tree, bird, or musical instrument. You are being asked to *imagine yourself* as a tree, bird, or musical instrument. The analysis of recurring patterns is important here, as is a true reading of the meaning of the metaphor. In the complex likenesses and interweavings of metaphor, a sense of the self emerges: not the self as expressed in conventional ways, but the true inner self, rarely expressed. You must be honest. "Though I think it's more respectable to be a well, I know I am a waterfall." In the difference between the reality and the wish, you can learn about the assumptions you were raised with; that you were expected to be hidden, motionless, silent, and available instead of open, exuberant, rapid, noisy, and a little dangerous.

You may be outraged or disappointed that, instead of a serious quest on the track of the immortal self, here we are, playing party games. Games are as good a path to self-discovery as any other, if you take them in the right spirit. And what is the right spirit? The spirit of play. Playfulness is no enemy of seriousness, nor is solemnity a guarantee of significance. So play--and learn from your playing. Give honest answers and don't take yourself too seriously. Joy is important, and it disappears the moment you indulge in self-importance. Satan--according to G. K. Chesterton--fell through force of gravity.

Smoke

Each word is a category of comparison. If you were a kind of weather, you would be _____. Fill in each space. If you find yourself torn between two possible metaphors, list both. Let some time pass before you try to interpret the results. When you reread the list of your metaphorical selves, you should look for patterns of response. Perhaps you find yourself similar to storms, wild animals, creatures of power and freedom, and untamed landscapes. Are you expressing that part of yourself? The game is meaningless without the hunt for patterns. When you find the significance of the varying metaphors, you will be coming close to the pure self, the individual, created spirit.

weather _____

tree _____

stone _____

plant _____

mammal _____

reptile _____

bird _____

insect _____

light _____

breeze or wind _____

planet _____

season _____

landscape _____

body of water _____

flower _____

vegetable _____

fruit _____

food _____

drink _____

form of government _____

nation _____

city _____

building _____

period in history _____

historical character _____

item of furniture _____

cloth _____

art form _____

type of music _____

piece of music _____

musical instrument _____

literary form _____

book _____

fictional character _____

language _____

culture _____

disaster _____

mythic creature _____

geometric shape _____

machine _____

metal _____

tool _____

ornament _____

profession _____

skill _____

sense _____

texture _____

smell _____

process _____

smoke _____

The Game of "Who Am I?"

In the three following exercises, you will be defining some of your qualities. It is an essential part of the grail-seeking process, and one that does not end here. In order to deal with what you want and need in work and relationships and what God wants from you, you should have at least begun to see and accept who you are.

The phrase *who you are* assumes that there is a continuity of some sort, and it is that continuity we are seeking. Your two-year-old self, your 20-year-old self, and your 57-year-old self look and sound and act differently, but they are all you. What is that mysterious selfness? The essential you; your spirit; your set of genetic instructions; the angles and placements on your horoscope wheel; your characteristic and unique reactions, talents, preoccupations, speed of thought.

This exercise works--that is, gives you some insight into yourself--if you can look at yourself honestly and speak the truth. Once again, there are no right or wrong answers, only truthful or untruthful ones. No one will judge you. There are no points to be added up at the end to tell you that you are sexually inhibited or too fond of gossip.

Nevertheless, you may have a hard time saying certain things about yourself. If you do, write about it in the journal. Discovering this kind of block is an important part of the process. What do you find so difficult to say? Maybe you feel forbidden to express the good things about yourself, either on general or specific principles ("Bragging brings bad luck"; "If I'm smart, the boys won't like me"). Maybe you have a hard time expressing certain taboo feelings or qualities ("I am not allowed to be dependent/independent/lonely/assertive"). Some taboos may be cultural in the sense that the broader culture forbids them; others may spring from your family or your private experiences. Once again, if you can identify the block, write about it.

In defining yourself, you may find essential (and perhaps unchangeable) characteristics that you hate. You are the wrong gender, or you are poorly coordinated, or your mind is mathematical when it "should" be verbal in trend. Perhaps you despise your inabilities--whatever you cannot do--or you devalue your abilities--whatever you can do.

The problem is not that you are unathletic or no good at English. The problem is that you have been brainwashed into hating yourself for being unathletic or no good at English. If you didn't care about how good you were, you would go on playing volleyball or reading poetry without worrying about the humiliation of missing a ball or a meaning that someone else caught. In other words, you would do the sport or the poetry for its own sake, not for the glory you get doing it. In doing so, you might get better. You may never win an Olympic gold medal or the Nobel Prize for literature, but do you really have to? Not if you participate for the sake of the activity itself.

Unfortunately, our school systems foster competition. Our parents urge us to glory in the fields they value, and our peers mock us for failures. But you can overcome the memory of that humiliation and shame. When you rouse such memories in the exercises below, write about them in your notebook. Purging the shame of being chosen last at games may be the first step to learning to love and accept your body. Learning to read--or sing or paint or dance or do logic problems or cook --simply for the joy of it can enhance your life in unexpected ways.

Adjectives: What Are You Like?

In the game of "Who Am I?" it is easiest to begin with adjectives. They describe you without defining you (as the nouns in the next exercise define you).

Write down ten adjectives that describe you. They should be the ten that best describe your essence.

Examples: *I am loving, generous, moody, eager, intelligent, passionate, solitary.*

I am _____

Nouns: Being

The adjectives described you; these nouns will define you. Think of this exercise as an equation: I = whatever. Though you are not really equivalent to any single aspect of yourself, some aspects are important enough to be essential to your vision of yourself. They can be related to work, play, private tastes, personal history, whatever is meaningful to you. Use nouns because you want to come close not to what you are in the process of doing (as expressed by "I am learning . . . thinking . . . feeling" or other present-perfect verbs), but what you are in your core. The next exercise will use the verbs.

Phrase your definitions positively, not negatively. Remember Nixon saying, "I am not a crook." Don't define yourself as a negative--"I am not a good daughter" or "I am not a success." Be honest, though; if you feel defined by something in yourself that you want to change, write it down. Later you can figure out a way to deal with it.

Examples: *I am a maker of metaphors.*
 I am a loving wife and friend.
 I am a pacifist.

I am _____

I am _____

I am _____

I am _____

I am _____

I am _____

I am _____

I am _____

I am _____

I am _____

Verbs: Becoming

What you are is important; what you become is more important. For years I was crippled by believing I could not change. Then I realized that I had been changing and could take charge, take control of my changes, and indeed be what I wanted. You can change, too. Find ten things in yourself that you are in the process of doing, learning, changing, and write them down here.

Examples: *I am losing weight by learning to trust my body.*
I am becoming more socially involved.
I am asking myself a lot of questions about how I should live.

I am _____

_____

I am _____

_____

I am _____

_____

I am _____

_____

I am _____

_____

I am _____

_____

I am _____

_____

I am _____

_____

I am _____

_____

I am _____

_____

THE WORLD AND THE FLESH

The body, our fleshly reality, tends to get short shrift in spiritual circles. Some faiths starve, beat, deny, or repress the body in order to save the soul; others simply ignore it. The general attitude tends to be that the exuberant flesh will assert itself anyway, while the frail spirit needs tender nurture. Worse, this attitude tends to be extrapolated from the individual level (each person's body) to the general (the world). Exploitation and destruction are the watchwords of this attitude. After all, the world is ours to "subdue."

This way of thinking is almost purely Western; no other culture treats nature as an alien, vicious, in need of sternly repressive measures. All too often, it masquerades as a Judeo-Christian value as well as a Western one. Yet the Bible speaks of nature and the natural world as being one way to seek and find God; the magnificent poetry of Job and the Psalms express the majesty and glory of nature. The Song of Solomon is a joyful, exultant vindication of loving sexuality, some of the most erotic poetry ever written. The flesh was created by God and doubly blessed when Christ took on the form--in the fullest sense of the word, all the aches and ills and solid material reality--of a man. Therefore, let us dismiss any notion that enjoying physical life is sinful or unspiritual or materialistic. There is a Talmudic saying that we will be held responsible after death for all the pleasures we failed to enjoy in life.

We are here, on Earth, and have no choice but to live a physical life until we die. You must come to terms with the physical world or die unsatisfied and incomplete. Moreover, you can find great joy and inner harmony through an acceptance of your own fleshliness. This acceptance is made even more difficult by another set of cultural values: the ones that dictate precisely what you should look like, and God help you if you are insufficiently tall or thin or white or young, if you are overendowed or underendowed (these words deliberately refer to a "standard" body we all are expected to strive for), or if your body is not lifeguard-healthy and strong. This issue tends to be of more concern to women, to minorities (who generally do not conform to the prescribed standards), and to persons who are in any way disabled. However, everyone can and should examine not only their attitudes toward their own bodies but also their attitudes toward those of others.

The first step in dealing with the world and the flesh is to define some of the issues involved. What exactly are we dealing with? See the list in Table 3.1. These issues are all part of the earth element (see Chapter 4 for more on the four elements).

Some people have little or no trouble accepting the physical realm. Others have a much harder time coming to terms with Earth; to them it means coming to terms with a difficult, dangerous, and forbidden subject. Most of us (including myself) are in the middle. Maybe you can deal with the issues of sexuality and gender but have a hard time accepting the fact of your mortality. Maybe you are comfortable with money and work but hate the way you look. Maybe you have systematically dealt with pain by eating or other physical overindulgence. Maybe you feel so guilty over pleasure that you have to punish yourself for it with exercise or getting sick.

These exercises will help you define your attitudes toward your body. You will see the areas where you are already strong and those where you need work. You will do some exercises to enhance your awareness of physical things, and you will learn to enjoy and use your own particular physical gifts. In such matters, however, theory is almost meaningless and experience is everything. Making changes in this area demands ongoing effort; just reading the section through will not endow you with permanent enlightenment about physicality. Practice every day; forgive yourself for failures; remember that persistence is an earthy trait, and that Earth splendidly rewards persistence. Above all: let yourself feel.

A Few Notes on Technique

Most of the techniques used in this book use the imagination and the intellect in conjunction with the physical act of writing down. Visualizing is easier and freer when your body is comfortable. Metaphors compare your spirit to things that are corporeal and solid. Though intellectual techniques can help you understand the power and mystery of your body, they cannot do the job alone. At some point you must allow the flesh to take over and sweep you away. In these exercises you will find specifically physical techniques along with the usual games, journals, and visualizing. The physical techniques use stones, dance, and your senses to take you into a place before words: Earth.

Before you can lose yourself in the flesh, you must pinpoint your current position with the help of the following exercises.

Awareness

What physical activities make you most intensely aware of being yourself?_____

_____

_____

_____

_____

What physical activities make you forget yourself? _____

_____

_____

_____

_____

Play "Who Am I?" with your body. Find ten adjectives to describe your body.

My body is_____

_____

_____

_____

Table 3.1: The World and the Flesh: Some Issues

the body
sex
gender
birth and parenthood
disablements and handicaps
sickness
aging
death
pain and pleasure
food
work
money
possessions
home
dependency
the environment
nature--animals, trees, rocks
the seasons
the world
time

The list of Earth issues in Table 3.1 represents the ways you manifest and deal with Earth energies. For each of them, go through the following list of questions. Respond honestly and thoughtfully, recording your answer in your notebook.

--What's your first memory of this?

--What's the best thing about this?

--What's the worst thing about this?

--What about this makes you feel joyful? angry? quiet? free? energetic? self-confident? frightened? lonely? trusting? eager? relaxed? brave? tender? loving? sad? awed? ashamed? despairing? peaceful? glorious?

--What single image would best express the way this works in your life?

Some Fleshly Exercises

Thinking about your body and your feelings about physical matters is useful but limited. The body keeps its secrets well. The following exercises should address fleshly issues more directly. You may choose to do a few of the following exercises, all of them, or one or two several times and in different circumstances. Some require one or more partners. Do not try to do all these at once; it may be overwhelming or confusing.

After you have done each, write about it in your journal, asking yourself how it really felt, how you expected it to feel, what connections it made in your mind. For example, you may feel physically sore after exercise or massage--which may be normal and expected--yet the soreness makes you feel angry, resentful, even ashamed. Why? Let your body tell you; let it make connections. You may then realize that your anger, resentment, and shame are the same feelings you experienced after being physically punished as a child. Then you must ask yourself how such punishment has affected your attitudes toward your body, toward authority, toward exercise, toward pain. Follow the strands of feeling wherever they lead.

Or--to take a more cheerful example--the dancing may awaken a sense of exhilaration and power in you. After enjoying and expressing that feeling, you should ask yourself what other things in your life make you feel that way. If nothing does, you should dance more often! The journal is not just for recording painful discoveries but for joyful ones as well. Use your journal to list things you love to do and want to do more often.

Dance Exercises

Dance alone to the music you like best. This exercise should be repeated often.

--Try dancing to different kinds of music: quick, energetic music; slow, languorous music; tribal music by Native Americans, Australian aborigines, or Africans; plaintive Celtic music; music for belly-dancers; Hebrew melodies; folk music of whatever country or culture; ancient Greek or Latin music; Gregorian chant.[1]

--Dance in front of a mirror. Praise your own grace and energy. Watch how marvelously your muscles move. Notice your expression: is it dreamy, intent, excited, afraid? Are you self-conscious?

--Dance naked (in front of a mirror or not). If you can (without getting arrested or disturbing others), try this outdoors in sunshine, wind, or rain. Do not get struck by lightning.

--Do any of these exercises with a friend or lover, or with several people whom you trust.

Bathing Exercises

We all spent the first nine months of our lives hovering weightless in warm water, and the sensation of being surrounded by water can help soothe us, promote meditation, and ease the expression of emotions. A bath is inexpensive, comforting, and good for you. Moreover, it is within the reach of virtually everyone who has a home. For those unfortunates who have only showers, see if you can borrow a friend's tub for the afternoon.

Here are some suggestions for bathing to promote meditation and relaxation.

--Fill the tub with water; just above or below skin temperature is good. Relax and begin to meditate. At a certain temperature--exactly skin temperature--your skin can scarcely sense the water.

Floating in water that temperature is almost like being weightless or unborn. What images fill your mind? Are you glad to be free of your flesh, or does this new freedom from stress and gravity make you feel more connected to your body?

--Do any of the exercises in this section in the tub. (Music and visualization exercises work especially well.) Does the warm, accepting environment make a difference? Are you comfortable with your nakedness? Instead of doing dance exercises, try slow gentle motions of the fingers and arms or the toes and legs.

--Try herbs or bath oils to scent the water. Which makes you feel most at peace? most sensual? most earthy? most spiritual? most cheerful? most healthy? most connected to the Universe?

--When you are tempted to do something you know is bad for you (smoke, overeat, take drugs, whatever), take a soothing bath instead. If that is not feasible, visualize yourself in a bath, surrounded by warm, loving water.

--Set aside time for a forgiveness ceremony. Make whatever bath preparations you like best, whether scented, herbal, or bubble bath. Bring in candles. By their light, bathe for a long time, dwelling on the beauty of your body. Meditate on forgiveness and cleansing. Pray for God's forgiveness and watch your sins float down the drain. Ask yourself for forgiveness for all the sins you have committed against your own flesh. Remember ways others have hurt your body. Now, in peace and safety, forgive them. Wash the shame away. Your body, created by God, can be clean and good. Thank God for the gift of flesh.

Massage Exercises

Techniques for massage are available in a number of excellent books. Here we are more interested in the psychic and emotional value of massage. Like dance and bathing, massage can make you more aware of your body and more accepting of it. It can promote meditation and remind you of suppressed memories or forgotten pleasures.

Massage almost always means having someone you trust put their hands on you. Self-massage can also be therapeutic, but for the sake of ease, we will assume that you are doing massage with Friend. Friend may of course be a professional massage therapist, chiropractor, or accupressurist. A caveat: If you have been raped or sexually abused, you may not be able to trust a masseur, even one who is a close friend. If you find unpleasant memories coming up from the pressure of someone else's fingers, skip this step and get therapy.

Here are some suggestions for massage to promote meditation and relaxation.

--Ask Friend to massage your feet and ankles. Spread your toes and feel their freedom from shoes. Feet usually hurt first, and if your feet hurt, your whole body hurts. Relieving that tension may make you feel better immediately. Try also the neck and shoulders, the hands, and the scalp. What do you think about when you are being touched? Is it enjoyable, or are you tense? Do you feel happily pampered, or are you uncomfortable with being served? Are you concerned that Friend will judge your body?

--Massage Friend. Rejoice in the texture of Friend's skin and muscles. Do you move rhythmically or are you jerky and uncomfortable? Does the effort of massaging feel good to you? Do you feel comfortable or uncomfortable with having power over Friend? Do you feel responsive to Friend's nerves and feelings? Are you judging Friend's body against some pre-set standard?

MEMORIES

Discovering yourself has, so far, focused on yourself in isolation: your spirit, your body, alone and inviolate. But no one exists in a vacuum. You live in relation to other people, to your own history, and to God, and these relationships must be explored before you can truly understand who you are. This section will deal with memories as a way of rediscovering yourself. You will examine who you are when you are with other people, how you have changed over time, how time and experience have changed you. Further, you will begin to see the patterns in all the exercises you have done up to now. There is no point to all the games, the exercises, the journals, if you do not begin to see a whole picture of yourself.

How does the memory of what you were in third grade affect you now? Do you act like your adult self with your parents? like a rebellious teenager? like an obedient child? By exploring and analyzing your key memories, you can begin to answer these questions about important relationships. Moreover, these relationships often echo and repeat one another: You may respond to your boss exactly as you used to respond to your high-school principal, and the way you feel about your mother probably influences the way you now deal with your mother-in-law. The search for patterns can help you understand and change the way you relate now.

A Few Notes on Technique

Stepping back into memories is a two-stage process. You must go back and feel them, see them as you did when they first happened, with all the freshness and vigor of real life. Record them in your journal with as much accuracy and passion as you can. Then--perhaps after allowing yourself to cool off for a while--go back to the memory and look at it with a new perspective. You must detach yourself from it. Look at it as an outsider would. Imagine what it would have been like if you had been another player in the memory. Walk back through the memory, imagining how you would feel, speak, and act if you were going through the experience now. Visualize different ways of dealing with similar situations.

These directions are obviously useful for unpleasant memories, but are they really necessary for pleasant ones? Yes. For illustration, let me offer an episode from my own life.

When I was very young, my mother used to tell us when it was exactly noon, so we could go outside and step on our own shadows. There seems to be nothing dramatic, nothing revelatory, about that memory. Yet it indicates as nothing else could how playful my mother was with us; she always found time on sunny days for that pleasant ritual. The circumstances of our lives then need investigating, too. She would then be just under thirty; she had four children under five years old, a full-time job and whatever part-time work she could gather, and a husband away at school. There was no extra money, no extra time or energy. With no adult companionship, with the heavy burden of poverty and isolation (we lived on a remote farm), with four young children needing her attention, she nevertheless remembered every sunny day that her little girls liked to step on shadows. That sort of daily heroism, that ability even in the worst of times to make everything into a party, is one of my mother's greatest assets. She passed that joy in little things on to her daughters. Thinking of those hard years, of her youth and isolation, makes it easy to admire her strength--and far easier to forgive her her mistakes.

Your own memories are filled with such treasures. It is time to discover them. The following exercises are designed to stir up memories. If the self has a certain continuity, it is at least partly based on memory. Theoretically, the brain remembers everything, whether or not you can consciously recall it. So it is in your best interest to discover what secrets your mind has been keeping from your emotions.

You may find it easier to use the techniques of visualization for these exercises. Relax and give yourself time not only to recall certain things, but also to feel them all over again. Then you can sit down at your journal to record the memories and what they mean to you.

For each of the memories evoked, concentrate on the following questions. Think about who was there; what you saw, smelled, heard, tasted, touched, thought, and felt; what happened immediately after or before. Is this memory a totally private one or a cherished family story? How old were you? Try to remember when it happened, both the time of day and the time of year. Write it all down. Then cool off, return to the memory, and consider other viewpoints, other circumstances. Visualize doing it differently. Write down your changed perceptions. You may want to use two different colored pens for the original memory and the analysis. It might also be a good idea to write the memory on the left-hand page of the journal and your comments on the right.

Working in batches seems best. Write down a number of memories about a single subject or dealing with a specific time in your life. Then cool off and come back detached, ready to look at everything from a different point of view. Remember, nobody's life is free of loneliness, shame, fear, guilt--and nobody's life is entirely miserable, either. Try to see both sides.

--What is your earliest memory? Have you always been able to recall this event? If not, when and how did you rediscover it?

--What are the three best memories of your life? What made these moments so special? Do the three have anything in common? If you were doing something that made you happy, do you still do it? If not, why not?

--What are the three worst memories of your life? What made these moments so painful? Do the three have anything in common? If you were in a situation that made you miserable, is it one that has come up again?

Certain relationships have particular power and importance. Recall an incident that sums up your overall relationship with the following people:

--Your mother

--Your father

--Each of your siblings

--Each of your children

--Each of your grandparents and other relatives who were important to you

--Your first love and any subsequent romances

--Your spouse(s)

--Your in-laws

--Your most-hated teacher

--Your favorite teacher

--Your most-hated boss

--Your favorite boss

--Your best friend (at each stage of your life)

Because many of these relationships change over time, repeat the exercise for different stages of your life. For example, your relationship with your parents probably changed, depending on your age and degree of independence, as well as any external factors. You may want to record half a dozen important incidents for each of your parents: one when you were extremely young, another when you were an active child, a third when you were an adolescent, a fourth when you first left home, a fifth when you married, a sixth when you had children of your own. In this way you can trace the changes in the relationship and identify areas of recurring conflict. Repeat the exercise only for those whose relationships have changed over the years.

Analyzing the Results

When you have completed the exercises, look for patterns in relationships. Did you react to your first boss as you did to your tyrannical sixth-grade teacher? Do you have the same problems with your best friend as you did with your sister? Does your spouse act like a sibling, a friend, a parent, someone else? Are you able to feel angry with your parents-in-law as you dare not be with your parent?

Looking at the individual relationships over time is also helpful. Perhaps you get along well with your siblings when all are equally happy and prosperous, but you quarrel and get jealous when one is especially honored or lucky. Perhaps your relationship with your mother was pleasant when you were a toddler and when you turned to her for advice after your first child was born, but marked with bitter quarrels when you left for college and when you showed your independence as a ten-year-old. Seeing the pattern here can make you understand how each relationship works, what is expected of you, and how you deal with conflict.

Moreover, you should be able to see others in your life--your parents, siblings, spouse, children--in a new way. Seeing in two lights is helpful. For example, when you recognize the pain and fear that drove someone to hurt you dreadfully and undeservedly, you will find it easier to forgive that person; at the same time, you still recognize that you did not deserve to be treated so harshly.

Seeing in two lights is an essential method for learning to love others as we love ourselves. When judging our own actions, we usually take into account moods, motives, health, and other mitigating circumstances; we should offer that mercy to others as well. Conversely, we tend to judge others' actions strictly as they affect us; we should judge our own actions by the effect they have on others. Seeing in two lights can help us realize that we, too, are sometimes cruel, unjust, or hurtful. Having faced our own potential for doing wrong, we can learn one of the most difficult of all lessons: to love the sinner and hate the sin.

SPIRIT AND SHADOW

The spirit is the mythic self, the part that worships and creates, that responds to art and myth. A life lived without discovering the nature and meaning of the spirit is a wasted and ultimately meaningless life. (In this section we will be dealing with the more mundane functions of the spirit. The relationship with God is dealt with more fully in Chapter 9.) The Shadow also belongs here, because the Shadow is a mythic character.

Discovering the nature of your spirit involves self-examination (of the kind we have been doing in journal entries and games), but it also demands reading, thinking, feeling, and ultimately recognition: yes, that is me in the mirror; that spirit is mine. In no other section is it more important to record your dreams. (Are you still following the directions given in Chapter 2?) Identifying the elusive spirit is essential.

Mythology and the Spirit

All your life you've been unconsciously choosing role models of one kind or another. Characters in books or on television and in movies, the gods and goddesses of ancient mythology, famous people you admire, even the Barbie or GI Joe you played with as a child--all of them gave you hints of how to act, talk, dress. They subtly guided your ambitions, your expectations, and your standards of right and wrong. From watching them, you learned what honor and courage meant, how to express anger and love, and how to deal with loneliness, humiliation, and death-- all by proxy, all vicariously. Your most important role models were and are your parents (or whoever raised you). This section, however, is concerned only in part with discovering what role models you have already chosen. You will also learn how to choose new myths and how to analyze the mythic content of any story, character, or trend. Once aware of their inner significance, you'll be far more in control of how they affect you.

Defining Personal Myths

Unfortunately, the word *myth* is often inaccurately used to mean a lie or contemptuously dismissed as an unscientific explanation of scientific facts. The wide-ranging and influential work of Joseph Campbell has done much to change the public's perception of myths as lies. A myth is the truth in the deepest sense, though it is seldom factual. It expresses the spirit behind the reality, the inner significance of external events. Pablo Picasso said, "Art is a lie that tells the truth"; the same definition applies to myths. They are metaphors for things that otherwise cannot be expressed at all.

Your personal myths are stories that you are drawn to because they express an important part of yourself or, perhaps, because they confirm the view of yourself that your parents gave you. If your self-image is essentially destructive, the myths you live by will be destructive, too. In that case therapy can help you remake your self-image and discover the myths that express your true self. These myths need not be--as one of my clients vividly put it--"a bunch of dead Greeks in togas chasing each other and turning into things." Fairy tales are one kind of myth. Novels and all the other forms of fiction can also be myths. So can what we think of as actual myths (tales of gods and goddesses, which are definitely worth reading if you have forgotten them), family stories, and even songs.

Myths, like literature, can be classed in a few convenient categories. Fleshed out by different plots and characters and dressed in a thousand possible styles, they come down to a few essential stories: the love triangle, the quest, and the coming-of-age, to name a few. The details are important, though, in the myths you live by. Realizing that your essential myth is a hero/quest tale is not as illuminating as understanding that the object of your quest is to maintain your integrity while gaining love. The essential shape of the myth is important, but so are the details; we will look for both.

Choosing a Myth

It may seem strange that I refer to your choice in the matter of myths and role models. Phrases such as "peer pressure," for example, imply that the self is a helpless victim of outside coercion. Adults can take responsibility for analyzing and changing their inner mythology once they have become aware of it--and once they become aware that change and choice are possible. In other words, you don't have to be a victim of what others did to you or expect from you or think about you. Freeing yourself is a long and painful process, but it will work.[2]

Children are more or less forced to accept their parents' view of things, but some children find ways to escape the relentless pressure, even violence, of their home lives. Children who survive disturbed families tend to find an outside role model, someone who cares for them. Or they may turn to books or daydreams to free them from misery. Teenagers try on a dozen different characters, looking for the one that fits them best and still lets them deal with their peers; that's why they are so unusually vulnerable to peer pressure. Teenagers with strong identities-- a powerful sense of self--are far less liable to give in to peer pressure.

One way to develop a strong sense of self is to exercise your choices in hypothetical situations. What if you discovered that your fiance had lied to you, deliberately tried to make you jealous, and attempted in a thousand subtle ways to dominate you--even trying to trick you into violating your most deeply held convictions? Would you have the courage and self-respect to leave, though you were friendless, poor, and desperately in love?

Jane Eyre did, and her staunch courage and indomitable will to be herself have provided a role model to millions of readers.[3]

Myths and Role Models

So far, I have spoken of myths and role models together. There are distinctions, however, that should be made clear. According to Joseph Campbell, "Myths are clues to the spiritual potentialities of human life."[4] In other words myths work on the deepest levels of the human spirit. On the other hand, role models may be quite superficial even though the ones you choose may tell a great deal about you. A role model is a real or fictional person whose actions, character, or other traits you admire or accept and wish to copy.

Some examples may help. Barbie was a role model for little girls of my generation; she shaped our expectations of what life was about--fancy dresses--and our image of what we would look like as adult women. Since few women have the figure of a Barbie doll, most of us are secretly disappointed in ourselves, since we have failed to measure up to our childhood fantasies. Jane Eyre is also a role model; early in the book that bears her name, she confronts her cruel aunt; later she leaves Mr. Rochester, since he has tried to destroy her self-respect. Throughout the book, her guiding principle is integrity; she will do nothing that soils and contaminates her own sense of self. Nor is she cold, selfish, and vain; she is gentle, spirited, and passionate, but she refuses to be compromised.

Fiction in general--even "nonliterary fictions" such as movies--is an essential source of myths and role models. Some fictions are specifically designed to be mythic; much good science fiction and fantasy works on this level.[5] The *Star Wars* trilogy is deliberately mythologized. But much great fiction works as a myth, without ever referring to elves, fairies, space ships, or dragons (and conversely, a lot of low-grade SF and fantasy is crammed with plastic dragons, fake insights, and no mythic worth whatsoever). The point is that you have to read selectively and become aware of the mythic patterns in your favorite fiction.

Good fictions take us through a mythic journey, and we learn unconsciously, the way children learn by playing with educational toys. It also helps to work consciously with myths. The exercises following will help you identify some of the mythic influences on you.

When you have finished, go back and compare your answers with the game Smoke and with the other exercises. If, for example, you've always been a loner, preferring to rely on yourself instead of sharing with others, it would come as no surprise if you tended to read lots of western or detective fiction. The same loner-hero appears in both kinds of writing. Watch for such patterns repeating themselves.

When I was young, my favorite story was _____

_____

because _____

_____

_____

If I could be a mythological character, I would be _____

_____

because _____

_____

_____

I always dreamed of being _____

because _____

_____

_____

I can't ever be _____

because _____

_____

_____

The Fairy Tale

Eric Berne said that everyone can tell the story of their lives as a fairy tale. That is true because fairy tales are a way of speaking symbolically about important psychological events: puberty, separation from parents, marriage, and death. Try to tell yours as a fairy tale. (Use your notebook if you don't have enough room.)

Once upon a time _____

_____

_____

_____

_____

_____

_____

_____

_____

_____

_____

_____

The Shadow

"Who knows what evil lurks in the hearts of men? The Shadow knows!"
The old radio serial tagline summarizes the role of the Shadow in your
psyche. But what is the Shadow? Where does it come from? How can
you deal with it?

If you think about what a shadow is, you can get a very good idea of
what the Shadow is. A shadow has the same silhouette as its object,
though it may be exaggeratedly stretched or foreshortened. A shadow is
two-dimensional and of one color (really no color), while its object is
three-dimensional and usually has several colors. A shadow is created
where light is blocked. You can never catch or touch a shadow. It looks
different at different times of day.

Thus the Shadow is created where light is blocked: by a lack of
acceptance. It is not a three-dimensional whole but a part, and it looks
different at different times of your life. But it always has your silhouette;
each Shadow is individual and unique.

The Shadow is not evil; it is the hidden, unloved, unaccepted side of yourself, and it knows things you have been told to forget.

> The shadow stands on the threshold between the conscious and the unconscious mind, and we meet it in our dreams . . . . It is all we don't want to, can't admit into the conscious self, all the qualities and tendencies within us that have been repressed, denied, or not used.[6]

Only by examining the Shadow can we understand our own potential for cruelty and creativity, for hunger and rage and shame as well as for kindness. Once we have accepted our own Shadow, we can learn to love our neighbors, forgiving them their trespasses against us because we admit that we also trespass. (Yes, facing the Shadow is linked with seeing things in two perspectives, as we did in the section on memories.) We can also learn to love ourselves, finding it possible to forgive our own sins--and accept God's forgiveness--because we have forgiven others.

Two kinds of things seem to be expressed by the Shadow: the real potential for doing harm, and those things the individual (shaped by family, culture, society) defines as wrong. Thus a person who believes deeply that sex is wrong and wicked usually places sexual acts in the Shadow, right next to rage and hatred. The Shadow contains anything in your self that is not acceptable to your self-image.

Everyone has the potential for cruelty, for theft, for lying, for adultery. For most people those things go in the Shadow. But other things may go in as well--things you need. If your parents emphasized neatness and punished or rejected you for being dirty (perhaps including in the category of dirt such healthy bodily functions as menstruation, elimination, even tears), you will probably (at least unconsciously) define yourself as a person who never touches dirt and someone who fears and hates germs as others fear and hate murder. But your Shadow will probably be full of forbidden dirt.

Fine. Let it stay there, with murder and adultery and all the other forbidden acts. The problem is that the Shadow isn't a locked trunk that safely stores all these forbidden things. The forbidden is still part of you; you must either face it in yourself or deal with it in some other way. Most often, it is projected and blamed on someone else. A woman whose Shadow is filled with dirt might wash her hands compulsively, seeing them as stained with guilt and filth. She sees dirt everywhere.

Other people are crawling with germs and must be avoided. Perhaps she blames other ethnic groups for not washing. At the same time, she would have a sick fascination for filth--perhaps symbolic, perhaps real. Depending on other circumstances, her reaction to the Shadow might range from being a neatnik to a full-fledged obsessive-compulsive disorder.

Often the Shadow itself--the forbidden thing--becomes an obsession. A prime example of the effect is the recent scandal involving certain televangelists. These men have, for years, defined sex as the chief immorality; they seem to loathe and fear women. In middle age, they were caught in sexual scandals. Most interestingly, one was accused by a colleague, condemned for very great wickedness and sin; the accuser was then revealed as a frequenter of prostitutes. The accuser was projecting.

What can you do with the Shadow? *Face it.*

If you don't face it, it will confront you anyway, though not perhaps in the dramatic way that it sent the televangelists toppling. By facing it you can turn it to use. Seeing your own capacity for wickedness--your own inner hatred, rage, greed, deceptiveness--you can prevent yourself from unconsciously acting out those taboos. (It is a basic law of psychology that we tend to act out whatever is taboo, at first in subtle and metaphorical ways and then in more and more direct ways, until the forbidden becomes the ritual. See the televangelists previously mentioned for an illustration.) Moreover, you will be able to understand and forgive others, and you may find vital parts of yourself trapped there. The lady with the dirt fetish, if she confronts her Shadow, will realize that she has for years hated herself because she is inescapably dirty: she menstruates, eliminates, cries, sweats. She can learn to love herself despite that; indeed, she cannot love herself until she sees it. Joanna Russ's short story entitled "The Little Dirty Girl" amply illustrates that issue.[7]

Many stories deal with a pure person confronting the Shadow. In the fairy tale "Beauty and the Beast" (much shortened and simplified), the Beauty lives with the Beast, who is very ugly and in some ways truly beastly as well, and learns to love him. Her love frees him from the spell of beastliness, and he becomes a handsome prince. They live happily ever after. In the movie *The Philadelphia Story*, Katharine Hepburn plays a proud woman who holds herself and everyone else to a high standard of conduct; because she cannot admit that she ever fails, she has wrecked not only her own marriage but also her parents' marriage.

When she is forced to face the possibility of her having lost control and violated her own standards, she learns to truly love others and becomes lovable herself.

Shadow Exercises

The exercises for discovering your Shadow will begin to put you in touch with the hidden side of yourself, one of the most important steps in the process of enlightenment. You will repeat some exercises from the section on the essential self and do some new exercises in visualization and journal-writing.

Smoke and Shadow

Play the game Smoke with your Shadow. As before, each word is a category of comparison. If your Shadow were a kind of weather, it would be _____. Fill in each space; if you find yourself torn between two possible metaphors, list both. Let some time pass before you try to interpret the results. When you reread the list of your meta-phorical selves, you should look for patterns of response. Perhaps you find your Shadow similar to storms, wild animals, creatures of power and freedom, and untamed landscapes. Are you expressing that part of yourself? The game is meaningless without the hunt for patterns. When you find the significance of the varying metaphors, you will begin to see how these fit with the essential self expressed earlier.

weather _____

tree _____

stone _____

plant _____

mammal _____

reptile _____

bird _____

insect _____

light _____

breeze or wind _____

planet _____

season _____

landscape _____

body of water _____

flower _____

vegetable _____

fruit _____

food _____

drink _____

form of government _____

nation _____

city _____

building _____

period in history _____

historical character _____

item of furniture _____

cloth _____

art form _____

type of music _____

piece of music _____

musical instrument _____

literary form _____

book _____

fictional character _____

language _____

culture _____

disaster _____

mythic creature _____

geometric shape _____

machine _____

metal _____

tool _____

ornament _____

profession _____

skill _____

sense _____

texture _____

smell _____

process _____

smoke _____

The Game of "Who Is My Shadow?"

In the three following exercises, you will be defining some qualities of your Shadow. This exercise works--that is, gives you some insight into yourself--if you can look at yourself honestly and speak the truth. Once again, there are no right or wrong answers, only truthful or untruthful ones. No one will judge you. It is easiest to begin with adjectives. They describe your Shadow without defining it (as the nouns in the next exercise define it).

Write down ten adjectives that describe your Shadow. They should be the ten that best describe your Shadow's essence.

My Shadow is _____

_____

_____

_____

Visualizing Your Shadow

Imagine your Shadow. Is it male or female, your own sex or the opposite? Does it look like anyone you know? Talk with it: What does it want? Whose voice does it have? What does it do for a living? Have you ever met it in dreams? Write down your visualization. You may also want to draw it or paint it. Write a journal entry from your Shadow's viewpoint.

NOTES

1. This may seem vaguely blasphemous. Gregorian chant is church music. My own fundamentalist upbringing taught that any dancing is wicked, for precisely the reasons I recommend it here: because it makes you and others aware of your body and may lead to sex. I do not wish to offend anyone, but I would like to remind the censorious that David danced before the Lord (2 Samuel 6:14). Dance can express praise and joy and beauty as well as simple sensuality; I think they are all good.

2. Once again, this book is no substitute for psychotherapy for people who have been deeply wounded. If your childhood has left you with scars, or if you were brutalized or raped as an adult, I strongly urge that you get professional counseling; it can help you heal yourself as no book ever could.

3. Charlotte Brontë, *Jane Eyre*. Available in dozens of paperback and hardback editions.

4. Joseph Campbell, *The Power of Myth* (New York: Doubleday, 1988), p. 5.

5. See especially the work of C. S. Lewis, *The Chronicles of Narnia* and the SF trilogy (*Out of the Silent Planet*, *Perelandra*, and *That Hideous Strength*); J.R.R. Tolkien's well-known Hobbit books; virtually anything by Ursula LeGuin, but especially *The Beginning Place* and *The Earthsea Trilogy*; Peter Beagle, *The Last Unicorn* and *Folk of the Air*.

6. Ursula K. LeGuin, "The Child and the Shadow," in *The Language of the Night*, ed. Susan Wood (New York: Perigee, 1979), p. 64. I wish I

could have quoted the entire essay; it is a clear, thoughtful exploration of the role the Shadow plays in our lives. For a less direct and analytical look at the Shadow, see some of LeGuin's stories, notably "Darkness Box" in *The Wind's Twelve Quarters* (Harper and Row, Publisher's Inc., 1975).

7. Joanna Russ, "The Little Dirty Girl," in *The Hidden Side of the Moon,* (New York: St. Martin's Press, 1987).

Chapter 4

The Power of Balance: Using the Four Elements

How shall we pass most swiftly from point to point and be present always at the focus where the greatest number of vital forces unite in their present energy? To burn always with this hard, gemlike flame, to maintain this ecstasy, is success in life.
--Walter Pater, *The Renaissance*

The earth does not argue
Is not pathetic, has no arrangements,
Does not scream, haste, persuade, threaten, promise. . . .
Closes nothing, refuses nothing, shuts none out.
--Walt Whitman, "To the Sayers of Words"

A being, breathing thoughtful breath,
A traveller 'twixt life and death,
The reason firm, the temperate will. . . .
--William Wordsworth, "She Was a Phantom of Delight"

The moving waters at their priestlike task
Of pure ablution round earth's human shores.
--John Keats, "Bright Star"

You have looked at your essential self, your relation to the world and the flesh, your memories and relationships, and your spirit's myths and Shadow. Those four areas of life correspond to the basic structure of the metaphysical Universe, the four elements: fire, earth, air, and water. Now it is time to look at the four elements themselves to see how they influence you individually and how you can keep them in better balance.

FOUR SPIRITUAL ENERGIES

The four elements provide the structure for most of the psychic arts. In astrology, they are manifested in three modes: cardinal, fixed, and mutable. Every sign is a unique combination of one element and one modality. In the Tarot, they are symbolized by the four suits. They can be applied to the ten sephiroth (branches) of the Tree of Life, one of the most ancient and powerful of mystic symbols. Understanding the four elements thus becomes extremely important to anyone interested in psychic work.

Since every schoolchild knows that there are 103 elements that make up all material things, how can a system that recognizes only four elements apply today?

It does--but you have to leave the realm of chemistry and move to metaphysics. Chemically speaking, the elements are not elements at all. Confusion arises because the same word is used for both, and the concepts are similar. Both chemical and metaphysical elements are basic components that are combined to form all imaginable structures and qualities. However, in chemistry the elements are physical; in metaphysics, they are spiritual. The four elements are symbolic ways of classifying the energies that, balanced or unbalanced, exist in all of us.

This classification is usually credited to Empedocles, a Greek poet, philosopher, and statesman who lived in the fifth century B.C.[1] However, the same classification is also used in India and China; it arose on every inhabited continent. Native Americans used the same formulation.[2] When the great psychologist (and occultist) Carl Gustav Jung looked at psychological types, he found four, which correspond with the four elements. (See the chapter appendix for a few of the many correspondences between the elements and other symbols, arranged by culture. See Chapter 7 for more information on the correspondences between the elements and the Tarot.)

There is clearly a strong spiritual truth involved here, one that, though it is no longer useful in chemistry, continues to be important to our understanding of the human psyche. Even our language owes a debt to the four elements; a person may be choleric (influenced by fire), phlegmatic (by earth), melancholic (by air), or sanguine (by water). These terms have changed their meanings over the years, but they originally referred to the four humors, the physical counterparts to the four elements. An overemphasis on one element would produce the condition of being choleric (hot-tempered and rash), phlegmatic (slow and cautious), melancholic (brooding and intellectual), or sanguine (cheerful and outgoing). Even modern slang uses the four elements, though in a derogatory way: hot-tempered, stick in the mud, airhead, wishy-washy.

What are the four elements? The simple answer is fire, earth, air, water. In the descriptions that follow, we look at the four elements in their purest forms. Bear in mind, however, that no person ever manifests only one element. Even an element that is woefully underrepresented is there; even one that is dominant is tempered by the presence of the others.[3]

FIRE

Fire is the spirit, the life force that drives all things to grow, flower, reproduce, and die. Though fire can be brilliant, it is by nature neither stable nor logical; instead, it leaps intuitively. Its intuition is not sensitivity to others' feelings, but rather an immediate grasp of an entire image, problem, or idea. Restless, seeking, passionate, fire knows only itself; in the light of its white flame, all things are revealed as spirit.

Fire is symbolized in the Tarot as the suit of Wands. In astrology the fire signs are Aries, Leo, and Sagittarius. Fire corresponds to Carl Gustav Jung's intuitive type.[4]

EARTH

Earth is related to the flesh and physical things, the embodiment and agent of thought, feeling, and energy. Earth holds and nourishes; what earth builds lasts. It knows by sensing--by direct perception of the world; earth sees and touches and smells and therefore is both sensual and practical. Receptive and stubborn, generous and strong, earth has an instinct not for feelings but of seasons and times. It is rooted in the slow cycles of the Universe.

Earth is symbolized in the Tarot as the suit of Pentacles. In astrology the earth signs are Taurus, Virgo, and Capricorn. Earth corresponds to Jung's sensation type.

AIR

Air is mind, the logic and intellect that create and spread ideas. The goal of air is to communicate. Because the basis of communication is exactitude, air analyzes and dissects. Unlike the passionate fire and the receptive, all-embracing earth, air is detached rather than self-contained. Communication requires more than one person, and so does love. Air is almost as restless as fire but less impulsive, though the two are similar in their endless seeking for knowledge (in the case of air) and experience (in the case of fire). Conversation, the intellectual sharing of thoughts, experiences, sensations, and feelings, is the realm of air, and it is conversation that binds us to each other more surely than any other tie.

Air is symbolized in the Tarot as the suit of Swords. In astrology the air signs are Gemini, Libra, and Aquarius. It corresponds to Jung's thinking type.

WATER

Water is linked with the soul, the gentle force that inspires us to worship. Feelings are essential to water, and water's intuition is sensitivity to emotion of all kinds. Fluid, responsive, giving, water is nevertheless both detached and indomitable. It responds, but its essence is unchanged; it escapes any attempt to destroy it, but gladly lets itself be captured. Water links us with the past through myth and with the future through prophecy.

Water is symbolized in the Tarot as the suit of Cups. In astrology the water signs are Cancer, Scorpio, and Pisces. Water corresponds to Jung's feeling type.

FINDING YOUR ELEMENTS

Having read the descriptions of the elements, you have probably already begun to sense which elements have the strongest impact on your life. But how can you tell for sure? The best method is astrology. At this point, you need to have an astrological chart.[5] You can, of course, check your local library for an astrological ephemeris and record all the planetary placements, but fast-moving planets may change signs, and you won't have your rising sign and house placements, which are crucial to understanding how your planetary placements work in your life.

Once you have a chart, look at it closely. It will show the placements of all the planets. List them here by sign and element. Remember that Aries, Leo, and Sagittarius are fire; Taurus, Virgo, and Capricorn are earth; Gemini, Libra, and Aquarius are air; and Cancer, Scorpio, and Pisces are water. I have included the symbols for each sign and planet so you can identify them easily. I have also included a weighting factor, which indicates how important or powerful the planet is.[6] When you start looking at which elements are dominant in your chart, the weighting factors will show where the strongest influences are; it is obviously more important that your Sun or Moon is in earth, for example, than that your Pluto is; everyone born during the 1960s (and some people born in the late 1950s or the early 1970s) has a Virgo Pluto.

Aries ♈	Taurus ♉	Gemini ♊	Cancer ♋
Leo ♌	Virgo ♍	Libra ♎	Scorpio ♏
Sagittarius ♐	Capricorn ♑	Aquarius ♒	Pisces ♓

VALUE	PLANET	SIGN	ELEMENT
4	Sun ☉	_____	_____
4	Moon ☽	_____	_____
3	Mercury ☿	_____	_____
3	Venus ♀	_____	_____
3	Mars ♂	_____	_____
3	Jupiter ♃	_____	_____
3	Saturn ♄	_____	_____
2	Uranus ♅	_____	_____
2	Neptune ♆	_____	_____
2	Pluto ♇	_____	_____

There are four other points that are especially significant in determining how the elements work for you. They are determined by the exact time and place of birth, so they cannot be placed unless you have a birth time.

VALUE	POINT	SIGN	ELEMENT
4	ASC Ascendant	_____	_____
3	MC Midheaven	_____	_____
1	Descendant*	_____	_____
1	IC Imum Coeli*	_____	_____

*The Descendant is the beginning of the seventh house. The Imum Coeli is the beginning of the fourth house.

Table 4.1: Astrological Rulerships

PLANET	SIGN
Sun	Leo
Moon	Cancer
Mercury	Gemini, Virgo
Venus	Taurus, Libra
Mars	Aries, Scorpio
Jupiter	Sagittarius, Pisces
Saturn	Capricorn, Aquarius
Uranus	Aquarius
Neptune	Pisces
Pluto	Scorpio

Once you have filled in all the blanks, you can start adding up. (The math is extremely simple.) Add up the number of points you have for each element--how many planets or points worth 4, how many worth 3, and so on. Then look at Table 4.1, the table of rulerships. *Add 1 point for each planet in its own ruling sign.* If you have the Sun in Leo, for example, add an extra point to the Fire column. If you have Saturn in Capricorn, add an extra point to the Earth column. Then figure out the total number of points you have per element. The element with the highest score is your dominant element, but do not ignore the other elements. They also influence you. Later in the chapter we will deal with the specific meanings of having different planets in different elements, having combinations of dominant elements, and how to balance the elements in your life.

FIRE   EARTH

FIRE

_____ X 4 = _____

_____ X 3 = _____

_____ X 2 = _____

_____ X 1 = _____

Subtotal _____

Rulerships _____

Total _____

EARTH

_____ X 4 = _____

_____ X 3 = _____

_____ X 2 = _____

_____ X 1 = _____

Subtotal _____

Rulerships _____

Total _____

AIR

_____ X 4 = _____

_____ X 3 = _____

_____ X 2 = _____

_____ X 1 = _____

Subtotal _____

Rulerships _____

Total _____

WATER

_____ X 4 = _____

_____ X 3 = _____

_____ X 2 = _____

_____ X 1 = _____

Subtotal _____

Rulerships _____

Total _____

INTERPRETING THE ELEMENTS: YOUR PERSONALITY

Now that the mathematics are done, you can start looking closely at what the results mean. There are two parts to this process: (1) discovering how your dominant element influences your life, (2) and discovering how each element affects individual planets and points. In later sections you will learn how to use elements to determine compatibility for romance, business, and friendship, as well as practical ways to balance the elements in your life.

Elements and Your Personality

The first thing to do when you have calculated your scores is to reread the basic description of the dominant element or elements. Then check the section that follows for the specific ways each element will make itself manifest in your personality.

FIRE PEOPLE

Fire people have a predominance of Aries, Leo, or Sagittarius in their charts. The essential principle of fire is *passion*. The word *passion* usually connotes sexual desire, but its full meaning is far greater. Passion refers to any powerful emotion, from love to fury; intense appetite, enthusiasm, or desire; and extreme pain and death, usually limited to the ritual suffering and death of Christ. The word passion comes from the Latin for suffering, and the word passion is related to the words compassion, sympathy, empathy.

Given this background, it is easy to see that fire people are intense about more than sex. Everything is intense to them. They seek out experience, direct or vicarious, and may make trouble for themselves if nothing is happening in their lives, just to keep their minds--and hearts--busy. They seek passion and are willing to suffer in order to avoid boredom.

Fire is fast, bright, attractive, occasionally dangerous; so are fire people. Their minds tend to work quickly, and they leap to conclusions with fine abandon. Just as people naturally gather around a blazing hearth ready to tell stories, they gather around fire people ready to hear stories. Unless there is a strong Scorpio elsewhere in the chart, fire people are anything but secretive; they love stories and tell them with relish. They love myths, symbols, metaphors, poetry, anything that promises intensity of experience. To them life itself is a staggering revelation. Their lives tend toward the dramatic. They have a passionate sense of self and of their own integrity. Violations of autonomy are not permitted; fire people will incinerate anyone who intrudes on their sacred personal prerogatives--space, independence, privacy, freedom.

Fire people's intensity can be self-centered. They are not usually interested in hurting others, but they may be so blinded by their own vivid experience that they never see someone else's feelings. They are quick to rage and quick to forgive; they may say or do unforgivable things in the heat of anger, but they may not understand why others remain hurt after the fleeting anger is gone. Their physical passions may also be fleeting; they are capable of falling in love in seconds, and may be ready to leave a relationship (having milked it of all its potential for intense experience) just at the time a slower person is beginning to make a commitment. That's how fire people got their reputation for being heartbreakers. Fire people cause themselves at least as much trouble as they do to others; their reckless disregard for common sense and logic, combined with their propensity to ignore the delicate emotional undertones of a situation, can lead them to disaster.

Fire people belong to Jung's intuitive type, meaning that they tend to see things whole, as in a brilliant flash of lightning. They are usually quick on the uptake (unless they have a slow, afflicted Mercury), but they may lack staying power. They are not primarily logical creatures. The connected chain of reasoning that logic requires is much more typical of air or even earth signs (especially detail-oriented Virgo). Fire exists in the now, and logic is too slow and too theoretical for fire's passion for experience and--that word again--passion.

EARTH PEOPLE

Earth people have a predominance of Taurus, Virgo, or Capricorn in their charts. The essential principle of earth is *strength*. Earth people are fascinated in one way or another with being strong. Their definition of strength includes practicality, prosperity, organization, and a surpassing ability to deal with real life. Solid, slow, steady, stoical--these words describe what earth people admire and exemplify. Their strength is not only the ability to endure passively, but also the strength to build and to defend. They have a solid sense of responsibility.

Being concerned with reality, they deal with constants: home, family, work, country, faith. Fads and trends rarely interest them, and they tend toward the conservative in outlook. Earth people are generally both kind and cautious; they can be nurturing, but only to their intimates. It may take years to be accepted by them, but they are loyal forever to those who earn a place in their hearts. They hold on with a bulldog determination to whatever seems good to them--and the past usually seems good.

Being so concerned with strength, some also become interested in power for its own sake. Possessiveness and power games (using emotional manipulation, subtle criticisms, or brute force) can be characteristic ways for an earth person to assert authority and ownership. Earth people may think of loved ones as their personal possessions, subject always to their will and desire; the discovery that the lover, friend, or family member has a will that opposes them is nothing more nor less than betrayal--the unforgivable sin. A fire person might slay you with a word spoken in sudden and unpredictable anger; an earth person may hold a grudge for years and get slow (often financial) revenge.

Earth people love good craftsmanship. They are natural materialists --not so much in the sense of being status-seekers, though some definitely prize worldly status--but in the sense of seeing the world only in terms of what can be touched, tasted, felt, seen, bought or sold. That is why they are called the "sensation" type in Jung's four personality types; they rely on their senses for their belief structures. They may have a natural, untaught spirituality that is linked with the slow revolution of the seasons and in essential pride in the craftsmanship of God. The world was obviously made and made well; that is their link to the Creator, and their service to God is also to make things well: to build families, homes, cities.

AIR PEOPLE

Air people have a predominance of Gemini, Libra, or Aquarius in their charts. The essential principle of air is *communication*. Air people think, communicate, analyze, and theorize. Their life is very much a life of the mind: detached, clear, unfettered. They love freedom and truth and clarity. They have a strong sense of justice and fair play, and they can be dispassionate and objective even when they might understandably be personally biased.

Air people can adjust with amazing speed to changing circumstances. Like cats, they always fall on their feet; they also share the independence and curiosity of felines. They love parties and meeting new people who might give them new ideas, and they can talk with anyone. Air people seek new ideas with vigor and energy; nothing so energizes an air person as a good intellectual argument, preferably over an abstract or theoretical idea.

Their devotion to the abstract can be their undoing; they may have a hard time making a commitment or sticking with one they have made. They love choices, lots of choices, and making a definite decision may make them panicky and claustrophobic. They can be elusive and maddening in argument, constantly redefining terms and shifting ground to prevent their opponent from addressing the real issues. Being articulate, air people can usually win with sheer technique even when they are wrong and know it.

Air people belong to Jung's thinking type. Instead of relying on emotion or intuition or practicality as their standard, they use rationality. This gives them their reputation for fairness; they judge cases dispassionately and on their merits, and they hold their friends and themselves to the same standards that apply to the rest of the world. This detachment may amaze a fire or earth person, to whom everything depends on the personal view. Their philosophical spirit enables air people to endure hardships and troubles by coming up with a rational explanation for it. They can endure anything as long as there seems to be a good reason for it, but they react with great anger to any unfairness. Air people tend to be crusaders for justice and for social causes of every description, whether or not the issue affects them personally. Not only do they crusade for others' causes; they are often the architects of change. They have the intellect and the philosophical background to theorize about new social orders, the articulateness to preach them and stir up the masses, and (with a strong Saturn or well-placed planets in earth signs) the leadership qualities to head up the revolution. As fire people seek passion and earth people strength, air people care about ideas and communication.

WATER PEOPLE

Water people have a predominance of Cancer, Scorpio, or Pisces in their charts. The basic principle of water is *sensitivity*. Sensitivity here means both vulnerability to emotion and sensing, being aware, being attuned. Unlike fire's passion, water's sensitivity to feeling is receptive rather than active. It waits, listens, receives, responds, in a simple unresisting fashion very unlike fire's defiant self-assertion. Water people feel the slightest vibration of the Universe; they sense the mythic meaning behind everyday reality and the deep emotions behind others' actions.

Water people have a surpassing awareness of spiritual realities and often seem to live more in the spiritual realm than in mundane reality. Everything they touch becomes sacred. Music, art, poetry, literature have special meanings for them. But water people don't just live in a dream world of art and beauty. They are deeply involved with other human beings. Water people nurture, tend, help; they are natural healers and often have psychic ability in addition to their supersensitivity to ordinary emotion. They can be tremendously loving and protective; everything in the world is alive to them, and they don't draw artificial boundaries around what deserves their love and what does not. Indeed, they have a hard time drawing boundaries between themselves and the world at all; they are the vulnerable heart of the world, as lacerated by a child's loneliness in Cincinnati as by the death of thousands in an Armenian earthquake.

Their very sensitivity is their worst problem. Strong earth placements can make them practical and solid; fire placements add a sense of self; air placements can give detachment. But unless these placements are very strong, the water person may become a victim of hypersensitivity. Water people may break under the sheer stress of feeling too much. They may seek escape through drugs, alcohol, or other addictions. Or, in sheer self-defense, they may construct a false, tough self that hides their true nature and enables them to deal at least a little with reality. The problem is that the toughness is a facade, and the painful emotions go on tormenting them in secret, finally manifesting themselves as depression or one of the addictions. Three things can help the water person in danger of drowning: a spiritual structure that gives them ongoing support; an artistic or creative outlet that allows them to act, not as the ultimate receptacle, but as the channel for emotion; and the will to look at all of reality--the good as well as the bad. Some water people are hypnotized by horror and pain because they are felt so strongly, and they forget to focus their attention on the joys of life.

Water people have a great gift of laughter and joy. They love intensely, all kinds of people: friends, family, lovers, strangers, people met in books. Water people know how to go with the flow of a peaceful day, simply enjoying life. Peace is important to them; they understand the great power of *satyagraha*, soul force, also known as passive resistance. They don't need to bluster and rant to get their own way; they simply move on, going around when they cannot go through, doing what needs to be done.

Balanced People

You may be one of the rare and lucky people whose elements are naturally balanced; your four scores are all within a few points of one another. Keeping the various areas of your life in balance may not be a problem for you; you have a reservoir of different methods for dealing with whatever comes up. Do check the next section, however, which will be most meaningful for you because it explicates how each planet operates in the various elements. You should find it quite illuminating.

INTERPRETING THE ELEMENTS:
THE ELEMENTS AND THE PLANETS

Each planet (or sensitive point) reacts differently to placement in each element. The brief explanations that follow describe the ways you will experience the combination of planetary and elemental energies in your chart. Four sensitive points are included here. The *Ascendant* is the first-house cusp; it is the sign that is rising at the time of your birth, and it deals with your self-image and the way you present your personality to others. The *Imum Coeli* is the fourth-house cusp; it is the sign at its lowest point at the time of your birth, and it deals with your home, your unconscious mind, and your mother. The *Descendant* is the seventh-house cusp; it is the sign setting at the time of your birth, and it deals with partnerships and marriage. The *Midheaven* is the tenth-house cusp; it is the sign highest in the sky at the time of your birth, and it deals with outward success, discipline, and your father.

PLANETS IN FIRE

The Sun. The Sun in fire is definite, assertive, enthusiastic, and lively. This placement adds to self-assurance and love of the dramatic. A strong sense of self is also indicated.

The Moon. The Moon in fire gives intense emotions and desire for experience, but it may lack sensitivity to others' feelings. It gives a love of entertaining and a desire for magnificent or unusual surroundings.

Mercury. Mercury in fire gives a great quickness of mind; it is not logical, but it is creative, vivid, and intuitive. A photographic memory is possible. It gives verbal facility, especially in storytelling.

Venus. Venus in fire adds passion, color, and vividness to love affairs. Men with this placement tend to look for exciting and dramatic women; women with this placement like to be seen as striking and passionate. It is not always conducive to maintaining fidelity or having children.

Mars. Mars in fire is aggressive and strong; this is a powerful and effective placement. The fiery temper is legendary, but this also gives directness and energy to every action. In men this indicates that they define masculinity as personal power and integrity; in women it indicates that they look for strong, energetic, and straightforward men.

Jupiter. Jupiter in fire gives phenomenal luck, the willingness and ability to make leaps into the unknown and come out ahead. This placement gives a jovial, generous, passionate tone to the whole personality.

Saturn. Saturn in fire represses risk-taking and spontaneity. The sense of self may be damaged, lessening self-confidence. It can add an element of common sense and responsibility to the personality.

Uranus. Uranus in fire is especially spontaneous, unpredictable, wild, and dramatic. It adds new energy and unexpected ideas to the sense of self; it can also mean broken relationships, insane risk-taking, and general instability.

Neptune. Neptune in fire offers a combination of sensitivity and passion that softens the fiery influence. Optimism and idealism are characteristic. Delusions of grandeur may also be possible.

Pluto. Pluto in fire transforms the self through intense sexuality, tests of courage, and a near-obsessive concern with self-image.

Ascendant. A fire Ascendant gives a need to be noticed and liked, confidence about physical appearance, and a powerful sense of self that may extend to self-centeredness.

Imum Coeli. A fire Imum Coeli gives a concern for dramatic and spectacular homes, perhaps also a certain restlessness. The mother may have been loving and spontaneous but not nurturing and protective.

Descendant. A fire Descendant gives a passionate marriage that may be without children. The intense concern for self may make partnerships difficult, but respect for the other person's space can create loving, vivid partnerships.

Midheaven. A fire Midheaven demands not just success but the appearance of success. Pride in work and in social position leads to the search for acknowledgment and affirmation. This native is trying to prove something by working so hard--probably to a flamboyant, critical, or overshadowing father.

PLANETS IN EARTH

The Sun. The Sun in earth is strong, practical, hardworking, concerned with achieving tangible results. It gives steadiness and the ability to endure. The primary concern is building something lasting and real.

The Moon. The Moon in earth gives a stubborn persistence of emotion. Feelings tend to be stable, slow-moving, not easily expressed. This placement gives a deep desire for a stable home and often a love for the land.

Mercury. Mercury in earth gives slow, careful thought. It may be analytical; it is certainly organized. This practical mind looks for the most efficient ways of doing things and achieving tangible results.

Venus. Venus in earth is careful in emotion until it feels secure. A stable, loving environment is essential. In men, they look for strength and sensuality in women; in women, they want to be seen as both practical and physically passionate.

Mars. Mars in earth gives a temper that is slow to anger and slow to forgive. Rage is not usually easily expressed, but it goes on hurting a long time. In men, they feel that practicality and good providing are the most important aspects of their role; in women, there is a desire for a man who is secure, stable, and sensual.

Jupiter. Jupiter in earth makes all physical things important. It emphasizes and often indicates worldly success, physical pleasures, and stable, traditional lives.

Saturn. Saturn in earth represses physical expression, often cutting off natives from their bodies. It breeds a dread of the real and may drive the native into fantasy. It may also give additional responsibility and seriousness about work and money, and gives a talent for organization.

Uranus. Uranus in earth revolutionizes the material world and the expression of the traditional. Money, work, and the body take on new and unexpected importance, but not in any way that is predictable.

Neptune. Neptune in earth infuses the real and mundane with dreams and ideals. Home, tradition, and success may be idealized and made more important.

Pluto. Pluto in earth offers regeneration through the real and the physical; health, money, tradition are seen as a way to transform the self in the symbolic death and resurrection. The reform of government, social institutions, and traditions are also indicated.

Ascendant. An earth Ascendant gives strength and stability to the whole chart; work, practical matters, and tradition are enhanced. A desire for the real and the tangible is common.

Imum Coeli. Earth in this placement emphasizes home, security, stability; it gives a deep love of the land or at least of the native landscape. The mother was probably the source of strength and possibly of financial support, though perhaps more involved with practical matters than the child's emotional needs.

Descendant. A steady, stable marriage is essential to someone with this placement. Physical passion cannot be unleashed without a committed and strong relationship. Though (or because) the native is selective in the choice of partners, marriages with these natives tend to be permanent.

Midheaven. An earth Midheaven cares about worldly success, making money, and achieving security. The practical and physical manifestations of work are most important. The father may have been unusually strict or repressive, respecting nothing but practical matters and scorning emotion.

PLANETS IN AIR

The Sun. The Sun in air enhances logic, clear thinking, and detachment. Communication of new ideas is most important to these natives, and they listen as well as they talk.

The Moon. The Moon in air gives a need to communicate emotion, to analyze and discuss it rather than experience it directly. The home must be balanced and harmonious, and any environment must give the native plenty of independence and room to expand.

Mercury. Mercury in air is a logical, intelligent placement. New ideas come swiftly, and old ones are dissected with analytic precision as well as absolute detachment.

Venus. Venus in air relies on talk to keep love alive. Communication is essential; it is the source and expression of passion. In men, the desire is to find an intellectual companion and friend who is also a lover. In women, there is a need to be valued for their minds as well as their bodies.

Mars. Mars in air expresses anger easily--perhaps more easily than it is felt. Analyzing anger may be easier than feeling it. In men, the conviction is that cool detachment and plenty of ideas are the meaning of masculinity. In women, there is a desire for a man who is intellectual, analytic, and detached.

Jupiter. Jupiter in air gives a broader philosophical basis to thought and communication, making good teachers and philosophers. It expands the mind and puts a high value on logic and detachment.

Saturn. Saturn in air gives an essential distrust of the intellectual and of logic; it represses original thinking and insists on tradition. It may also give responsibility and practicality to someone otherwise inclined to be too theoretical.

Uranus. Uranus in air changes communications and modes of thought. Wild new ideas come in; rationality is traded in for innovation. It gives original ideas to unusual people.

Neptune. Neptune in air enhances thinking about ideals and illusions. It may cloud thought or allow people to think in spiritual ways about logical issues.

Pluto. Pluto in air seeks to transform the self through the intellect. New ideas and technologies offer ways to enhance logic and theories. The self undergoes symbolic death and resurrection through changing the way the mind perceives the world.

Ascendant. An air Ascendant gives logic and intellect to the chart, emphasizing communication skills and abstract ideas. The need to speak, hear, know, and understand is overwhelming.

Imum Coeli. Air in this placement gives a need for intellectual stimulation at home. A balanced, pleasing environment, lots of independence, and others to talk with are important. The mother may have been distant, more interested in abstract thoughts or theories than the child.

Descendant. Air in this placement demands a marriage of two minds. Passion and commitment come from intellectual sharing, and the relationship itself is based on total sharing of thoughts. This may be an unstable placement; once all thoughts are shared, the native may move on to a new partner. The partner must be intellectually inventive and communicative for this union to last.

Midheaven. An air Midheaven seeks worldly success in order to get ideas spread and believed. Great communicative gifts and new ideas are common. The father may have been distant, involved in theories rather than in offspring.

PLANETS IN WATER

The Sun. The Sun in water gives an overall sensitivity, an awareness of emotional and spiritual realities beyond ordinary life. This placement gives natives a sense of the spiritual meaning of every act and thought, so that nothing is done from practical reasons but for spiritual or emotional ones. Essentially selfless and devoted to ideals or a mystical vision, the Sun in water may set aside personal ambitions for the glory of higher spiritual truths.

The Moon. The Moon in water is the most sensitive and emotional placement; this person, above all others, is affected by feelings, intuitions, atmospheres, with deep unspoken desires both to nurture and to be nurtured. Loving as it is, the Moon in water is also capable of hiding its sensitivity behind a tough shell.

Mercury. Mercury in water makes thought almost a form of feeling. Conversation, communication, and thinking all center around the spiritual and emotional. A quick mind is usual, but not a detached or analytical one--though emotion itself may be analyzed.

Venus. Venus in water values a harmonious and spiritual environment, with emphasis on the inner meaning of things and the spiritual aspects of love. In men, there is a deep desire to find meaning and spirituality through women; in women, there is a need to be seen as a spiritual and emotional person.

Mars. Mars in water is made gentle or (in the case of Scorpio) at least subtle. Aggressive emotions and a touchy sensitivity to insult are common. In men, there is a tempering of masculine aggression and acceptance of the feminine side of themselves; in women, there is a desire for a gentle, sensitive man.

Jupiter. Jupiter in water expands emotion, but may also make it philosophical and a little more detached. It gives a strong sense of religion or spirituality as the source of all the meaning in the Universe. This vision of creation as a whole and magnificent expression of the Creator's love is a sustaining force for those with this placement.

Saturn. Saturn in water makes it hard for the native to express emotion; the native may be ashamed of intense feeling or unable to come to grips with it, preferring to present a shell of competence. It may add an element of emotional strength and stability as well.

Uranus. Wild, uncontrollable emotion and psychic intuitions floating in from the Universe mark this placement. It stimulates new forms of emotional expression and an increased interest in psychic and spiritual matters.

Neptune. Neptune in water is an intensely emotional placement. Dreams, wishes, and ideals become tied to higher spiritual realities--or perhaps to the oversensitive self, in which case they may be seen as threatening and terrifying.

Pluto. Pluto in water offers regeneration through emotional and spiritual experience, the symbolic death and resurrection of the soul through deeply held convictions or ancient rituals. It may demand the sacrifice of what is held most emotionally dear, which will, of course, be resurrected in a new form.

Ascendant. A water Ascendant filters the whole world, the whole personality, through awareness of the spiritual and emotional truths beyond ordinary experience. Extraordinarily sensitive and aware, responsive to music and art of all kinds, this is a creative placement.

Imum Coeli. Home, mother, the spirit, are all sources of deep feeling in this placement. A highly emotional, nurturing, and protective mother is usually indicated, as is a desire for a loving and beautiful home.

Descendant. This placement makes partnerships more than a business arrangement; they are a search for the perfect soulmate who will understand and accept everything. Religious and emotional compatibility is essential.

Midheaven. The water Midheaven cares very little for worldly success but a great deal for spiritual and emotional satisfaction. The father may have been overemotional, perhaps an addict of some kind, making this native wary of emotional explosions.

COMPATIBILITY AND THE ELEMENTS: SOME PRINCIPLES

Most people are compatible with others who share their dominant element, but mixing elements becomes more complicated. The sections that follow give specific details about the problems and pleasures that different combinations can bring.[7]

The traditional principle is that, in general, fire and air people get along, as do water and earth people. Fire and air are active or masculine, earth and water receptive or feminine. This principle does work, but other combinations, though more difficult, may offer rewards. The air person may not have a natural affinity for the water person, but nevertheless may find life enriched by the mystical and emotional vision that the water person offers. Such combinations are dealt with in detail in the following sections.

Another factor to take into consideration is that few people--just about nobody--have only one element dignified. Most people have two strong elements and two weaker ones, or three strong and one weak, or even (a lucky few) a balanced chart. (These latter people must pay more attention to planets and points in various elements to determine compatibility.)

Perhaps the best combination of all is between partners who have one dominant element in common, and the other complementary. For example, Antonia and Julian, a very happily married couple, share a strong fire element, so they can easily understand each other's lively, enthusiastic natures, their passionate pride in their individual integrity, and their intuitive grasp of reality. Tony has a strong earth element, making her determined, home-loving, and practical as well as fiery. Julian's water element--which is, of course, compatible with earth--gives him a rare sensitivity and a need for the security of the steady love and the comfortable home Tony offers.

The combination would also work well with two water or earth people, one of whom had a strong fire, the other a strong air; two air people, one of whom had a strong water, the other a strong earth; and so forth.

Kinds of Relationships

Naturally, different kinds of relationships must be looked at in different ways. Charts can be compared to check on compatibility for a multitude of reasons, but romance and business are the most common, and these will be the focus here. You may also find it interesting to compare the element charts of family members: you may discover the source of hidden similarities and disruptive differences.

Love Elements

If you are looking for romantic compatibility, look for a dominant element/secondary element compatibility, as described previously in the case of Antonia and Julian. Whatever other elements are present in the chart, though, certain contacts are considered important. Check the male's Venus and Moon (his expectation and experience of women) against the female's elements in these planets. Check the female's Mars and Sun (her expectation and experience of men) against the male's elements in these planets. Then cross-check: his Sun and her Moon; her Sun and his Moon; her Venus and his Mars; his Venus and her Mars. These need not all be compatible, but there should be some degree of harmony between them. (Check the specific listings that follow for the effects of various element combinations.)

The Descendant's element for both partners should also be considered in order to discern the basic attitudes toward partnerships and marriage. A Descendant in the same element as the partner's Sun or Moon is very helpful; a woman's Descendant in the same element as the man's Venus is helpful too, as is a man's Descendant in the same element as the woman's Mars.

These methods of comparison are not confined solely to heterosexual couples. Both lesbians and gay men should compare their Sun, Moon, Venus, and Mars placements with those of their mates, as well as doing all the cross-checking advised above. A compatible Descendant is especially helpful; societal pressures often work against lasting homosexual relationships.

Business Elements

For business partnerships compare the partners' Midheaven (for styles of success), Mercury (for ways of thinking), Saturn (for self-discipline), and Jupiter (for expansion and blessing), as well as the Descendant (for partnerships). Second-house and sixth-house cusps may also be important; the second house deals with money and possessions, and the sixth with employers and employees.

When entering any business, alone or with a partner, you should check the element placement of the planet and sign that rule the activity under consideration. This will tell you how you will approach the activity. The healing arts, for example, are ruled by Mercury and Virgo, and publishing is a Sagittarian activity. (These correspondences are listed in many astrology books.)

Be careful not to limit yourself to traditional classifications, however. Few activities belong completely to one sign. To return to our examples, such modern medical techniques as radiology, CAT scanning, and electroencephalography are clearly Aquarian: they are high technologies designed to help people, but the doctors and technicians who perform these procedures or do the original research are distant, set apart from the sick people who need the help. (You might confide personal problems to your family doctor, but would you tell your troubles to your radiologist?) These Aquarian techniques heal without the messy personal involvements of traditional medicine.

Likewise publishing, which is generally a Sagittarian activity, also involves the intensely Virgoan and Mercurial process of copy editing, which involves reading a manuscript for sense, grammar, factual accuracy, typographical errors, repetitions, flawed arguments, and perfect footnotes (in the proper form, with complete information, and in the right order, with no omissions or duplicated numbers). That step is necessary for the Sagittarian spreading of knowledge, but it is pure Virgo. In addition, the subject matter helps determine the influence: Publishing books about armaments and military strategy is a Martian activity, while virtually all business books are Capricornian.

Since everyone has these planets and signs somewhere in the chart, you should make sure the element you have in that placement is compatible with your business plans--and with your partner's placements.

Element Compatibility

These combinations refer not only to separate persons with each element dominant, but also to parts of your own personality. The person who has both fire and earth emphasized in the chart will have some of the same inner conflicts that trouble a Leo married to a Virgo--and also some of the same strengths.

FIRE COMBINATIONS

Fire/Fire. This combination is perhaps best expressed by the phrase "fighting fire with fire." Two fire people will be able to understand each other intuitively, with none of those slow explanations so irritating to the quick fiery temperament. Both are likely to feel they have found, at last, the soul mate who understands their every thought and feeling. Their mutual enthusiasm and passion will burn brightly. Yet this is not an entirely stable combination; both are proud, touchy, and volatile, and they may not be able to maintain a steady relationship.

Fire/Earth. This is not one of the traditionally compatible relationships. The fire person may become impatient with the slow, cautious earth person, and the earth person may nurse hurt feelings from the fire person's quick temper. Yet, if they can learn to respect each other's unique talents and styles (the dash, brilliance, and imagination of fire; the strength, efficiency, and precision of earth), these two can complement one another. Earth helps fire turn dreams and visions into solid reality, and fire gives earth speed, intuitiveness, and enthusiasm.

Fire/Air. This is one of the traditionally good element combinations. Both elements are positive, restless, quick. They can converse far into the night on every imaginable subject, air providing the logic and fire providing enthusiasm and wild ideas. The fire person may become impatient with the cool detachment of the air person, and the air person can be scorched by the fire person's immediacy and intuition. Nevertheless, the fire person benefits from the air person's ability to theorize, and the air person may warm up when exposed to the fire person's passion.

Fire/Water. This combination can be emotionally shattering or blissfully intense, because fire and water are the most emotional elements. Fire can diminish water's delicate self-esteem without ever noticing that the water person is hurt; water can quench fire's enthusiasm by its insecurity and fearfulness. Fire offers water courage, energy, and a strong sense of self;

water can give fire a needed gentleness and an awareness of the sacred. Both see beyond ordinary, practical realities to their ultimate resonances.

EARTH COMBINATIONS

Earth/Earth. Words like *solid, stable, strong* describe this combination. Two earth people will understand and applaud each other's practicality and efficiency. Earthy sensuality is also a bond, and this union is likely to produce children. Though it may lack an element of vision and excitement, this relationship is likely to be permanent, because both partners hate change and seek security. If a breakup occurs, it may be caused by both partners' stubbornly holding on to hurt feelings; earth tends to nurse a grievance and rarely can see another's point of view.

Earth/Air. Earth and air is not a volatile--or exciting--combination. It can be a successful one, however. Earth's steadiness and practicality can ground air's theorizing, and air's detached and intellectual mind can help earth see things from new perspectives (earth usually has only one viewpoint: its own). If it fails, it fails because earth and air have few natural points of contact. They think, feel, and act so differently that there simply may not be enough in common for them to share or even to bring them together in the first place.

Earth/Water. A traditionally good combination, earth and water complement each other beautifully. Earth offers the stability and security that water craves, and water's sensitivity helps mute earth express its deep but silent feelings. Earth's practicality and (sometimes) materialism may bother water, which is spiritual and emotional in focus, and earth may be impatient with water's sensitivity to hurt and (sometimes) its daydreamy inability to ever get anything done. Nevertheless, a strong and fertile combination.

Earth/Fire. The earth person may nurse hurt feelings from the fire person's quick temper, and the fire person may become impatient with the slow, cautious earth person, Yet, if they can learn to respect each other's unique talents and styles (the dash, brilliance, and imagination of fire; the strength, efficiency, and precision of earth), these two can complement one another. Earth helps fire turn dreams and visions into solid reality, and fire gives earth speed, intuitiveness, and enthusiasm.

AIR COMBINATIONS

Air/Air. Air meets air in a rush of words. This combination can work beautifully because each partner has an instinctive understanding of how the other's mind works--and mind, of course, is what matters most to an air person. Even if they didn't understand each other, they soon would. Air constantly explains itself in words, analyzing actions, thoughts, and feelings. Another air person gladly listens and participates in such self-analysis, offering in return the same kind of analysis. If anything can make this relationship fail, it is the piling up of practical and mundane details--from housework to decision-making--that neither partner wants to deal with.

Air/Water. Air and water is a traditionally stormy partnership. Air is detached, cool, logical; water is involved, emotional, sensitive. The air person's abstractness can hurt the water person, who feels personally slighted, and the water person's emotional sensitivity irritates the cool and collected air person, who would like to discuss ideas rationally, without a personal application. Yet the partnership can work; the air person may learn to simply experience life, to give up the self to the sea of emotion, to see beyond the world of facts; the water person may learn to be detached, to communicate feelings in words, and to think of the world in logical rather than mystical terms.

Air/Fire. This is one of the traditionally good element combinations. Both elements are positive, restless, quick. They can converse far into the night on every imaginable subject, air providing the logic and fire providing enthusiasm and wild ideas. The fire person may become impatient with the cool detachment of the air person, and the air person can be scorched by the fire person's immediacy and intuition. Nevertheless, the fire person benefits from the air person's ability to theorize, and the air person may warm up when exposed to the fire person's passion.

Air/Earth. Earth and air is neither a volatile nor exciting combination, but it can be successful. Earth's steadiness and practicality can ground air's theorizing, and air's detached and intellectual mind can help earth see things from new perspectives (earth usually has only one viewpoint:

its own). If it fails, it fails because earth and air have few natural points of contact. They think, feel, and act so differently that there simply may not be enough in common for them to share or even to bring them together in the first place.

WATER COMBINATIONS

Water/Water. Water with water makes for an intense relationship. They understand one another, and they can avoid the slights and emotional wounds almost inevitable when a water person is joined with someone of a different element. This combination has its flaws, however. One water person may not offer much stability to another water person; indeed, the emotional intensity of such a union may be too much for one or both partners. Addictions or co-dependent relationships may flourish. Yet the mystical and emotional bond between two sensitive water people can be intense; this is the true love of the fairy tales, a merging of selves.

Water/Fire. This combination can be emotionally shattering or blissfully intense, because fire and water are the most emotional elements. Fire can diminish water's delicate self-esteem without ever noticing that the water person is hurt; water can quench fire's enthusiasm by its insecurity and fearfulness. Fire offers water courage, energy, and a strong sense of self; water can give fire a needed gentleness and an awareness of the sacred. Both see beyond ordinary, practical realities to their ultimate resonances.

Water/Earth. A traditionally good combination, earth and water complement each other beautifully. Earth offers the stability and security that water craves, and water's sensitivity helps mute earth express its deep but silent feelings. Earth's practicality and (sometimes) materialism may bother water, which is spiritual and emotional in focus, and earth may be impatient with water's sensitivity to hurt and (sometimes) its daydreamy inability to ever get anything done. Nevertheless, a strong and fertile combination.

Water/Air. Air and water is a traditionally stormy partnership. Air is detached, cool, logical; water is involved, emotional, sensitive. The air person's abstractness can hurt the water person, who feels personally slighted, and the water person's emotional sensitivity irritates the cool and collected air person, who would like to discuss ideas rationally, without a personal application. Yet the partnership can work; the air person may learn to simply experience life, to give up the self to the sea of emotion, to see beyond the world of facts; the water person may learn to be detached, to communicate feelings in words, and to think of the world in logical rather than mystical terms.

BALANCING THE ELEMENTS

If you have an element imbalance--and almost everyone does, to one degree or another--how can you create a balance in your life?

Your elements influence your choice of activities, your way of thinking, your patterns of emotion. Though you cannot change these realities, you can learn to stretch your range by trying activities that belong to the elements not dignified in your chart. Whether or not it is dignified by a planet or sensitive point, every element is placed some-where in your horoscope wheel, and you need to be able to express its energies.

Another use of element balancing is for those who have a strong element in their chart that they have learned to reject. Many people have a hidden side of themselves that, for any of a number of possible rea-sons, they have never expressed or been permitted to express. A client of mine with an overwhelming majority of earth in her chart had always devalued that domestic, practical side of herself as a way of rebelling against her controlling parents, who emphasized material success above all else. But she threw the baby out with the bath water and turned against her own nature. After a number of balancing sessions, she learned that she could express her earth without conforming to her par-ents' materialism. On my advice, she began doing things with her hands, particularly molding clay (a very earthy activity). Now, more in touch with her earthy side, she is selling her dragon sculptures at craft fairs and through gift stores. Another client had accepted his family's definition that water matters--music, emotion, religion--were strictly for women and sissies. He learned to accept his watery side and began to take great joy in music and art. At the same time, his tensions eased and he was able to cut back on several addictive behaviors that had previously been his only channel for emotion.

The key to balancing elements is to discover what activities express each element. Then practice them. It may be difficult at first; someone with little air or with unexpressed air may find it hard to be objective, to analyze ideas or feelings in writing, or to do other air activities, but with perseverance air can be expressed and the balance found. Some suggested activities for balancing each element follow.

Balancing Fire

Balancing fire entails expressing your true self. The metaphor game Smoke, already played, is a fire activity. Dancing (though a physical activity mostly belonging to earth) can also help you release your fire: dance energetically to music that makes you feel wild, loose, exhilarated. Go out into the rising wind of storms, feeling the crackling excitement of movement, disturbance, change. Visualize yourself as fire itself, as anything free, wild, dangerous, powerful. Feel in yourself your own white-hot core of passion. Visualize yourself in states of fire: in passionate love, in sexual frenzy, in rage. Glory in your own strength. Take calculated risks: go on an Outward Bound program, whitewater rafting, rock-climbing, riding horseback. Every day, try to do at least one little thing that makes you aware of the blazing original self in you, something perhaps not even on this list that makes you aware of your own heat and passion and aliveness.

Balancing Earth

Balancing earth entails becoming involved with the real. Because it is so physical, it is easier to list earth activities than those of any other element. To get in touch with your earth, do things with your hands: plant and tend a garden, bake bread, carve wood, mold clay into pots or statues (or just mess around with it). Earth needs visible results and expects things to take a long time; try to find an activity you find satisfying over a period of time so you can tap into earth's sense of process. Gardening is the archetypal earth activity. Get in touch with your own body as well: walk, exercise, stretch, feel. Become aware of the passing seasons and the changes in the world around you. Learn to be part of the cycle of the Universe. Every day, as you cook, clean house, and do other earthy chores, make yourself aware of their significance, not just to yourself. The cooked food will keep you alive, the cleaned house is an outer expression of the inner self--but also in joining you with the generations who have likewise cooked and cleaned and lived through the seasons. That unity is an essential aspect of earth.

Balancing Air

Balancing air entails learning detachment, communication, rationality. The archetypal air activity is breathing; it is no coincidence that breath is the material we sculpt into talk. To get in touch with air, breathe deeply in on a count of eight; breathe slowly out to the same count. Deep breathing calms and soothes; it enables you to take a more objective look at the world, which is another air function, and it clears the mind for creative thought. Write down your ideas, memories, and new experiences in a journal; try to express them clearly, and then look at them from a new perspective. Look for patterns in what you write and think. Analyze changes. Test out new ideas by discussing them with others or by thinking through all possible ramifications. Keeping a journal and keeping up friendships with conversation are daily necessities. Learn to be comfortable playing with ideas, looking at common things in a new light, discussing and analyzing concepts, creating new theories. To get in touch with air, breathe, talk, think, write.

Balancing Water

Balancing water entails getting in touch with your spiritual, emotional side. The best water activity is, of course, worship of God. Prayer, praise, and religious ritual offer a strong framework for expressing and deepening your awareness of water. On a more mundane level, you can balance water by learning to feel and to accept your feelings. If you are joyful, rejoice; enjoy every bit of that joy. Smile, let yourself be happy. If you are angry, just be angry; that may be frightening, but it's okay; it won't eat you. If you are grieved and weary, weep. If you are really sad, sit in the bathtub and cry--it takes you right back to the womb. These emotions are natural, right, real, and if you close them off, they will find another way to emerge.[8] Allow yourself solitude in which to meditate. Let peace and beauty in by looking at the beautiful world or at paintings. Read poetry. Listen to music every single day. Try singing, playing an instrument, writing poetry, painting pictures, to express how you feel. Walk along the shore of the ocean, a lake, a river. Let the water, restless or still, soothe your heart.

NOTES

1. *Brewer's Dictionary of Phrase and Fable*, rev. Ivor H. Evans (New York: Harper and Row, Publishers Inc., 1970), p. 369.

2. Barbara G. Walker, *The Women's Encyclopedia of Myths and Secrets* (New York: Harper and Row, Publishers Inc., 1983), pp. 272-276. A few cultures add a fifth, inert element--ether--to the list of four, but it usually only deals with the immortal soul and does not interrelate with other elements. The Taoists developed a five-element theory (often simply referred to as Chinese). It is complex and beautiful and used in acupuncture.

3. Classically, air and fire were known as "masculine" because they were active, while water and earth were known as "feminine" because they were receptive. Such classifications are both deceptive (they have no relation to what masculine and feminine really are) and destructive (dividing people into arbitrary categories not only can cause untold pain for those who do not fit, it can stunt and maim those who force themselves to fit). This system is descriptive, not prescriptive. However, the yin/yang, active/receptive categories do still have meaning. I have classified the elements using these terms instead of the emotive and inaccurate "masculine" and "feminine."

Everyone incorporates active and receptive qualities in the psyche; everyone is influenced by all four elements. It is not possible to be born without some of them. Even if one or perhaps two are not dignified in your astrological chart, they do and must appear in the twelve houses of the horoscope. Everyone has all the signs placed somewhere in his or her chart; that's why a full astrological chart is so much more revealing than a bare sun sign. In the Tarot it is rare for any reading to turn up cards of one suit only. Though a querent may show up as the appropriate card for his or her age and sun sign element, it's equally likely that the querent will show up as a different card in different situations, depending on the role played in that situation.

4. All the psychological types are to be found in C.G. Jung, *Psychological Types*, translated by H.G. Baynes, revised by R.F.C. Hull (Princeton, N.J.: Princeton University Press, 1971), pp. 330-407.

5. A basic horoscope wheel, identifying placements but without any interpretation, is available for $5.00 from me. Send check or money order to Kelynda, P.O. Box 201, Clifton Heights, PA 19018. Include your name, mailing address, daytime phone number, birth date (month, day, and year), birthplace (city, county, state, country), exact birth time if known (including time zone). Allow two weeks for delivery, though most charts are returned within three days of receipt. You can also write for a list of astrological, numerological, and other services and their prices.

6. The idea of a weighting chart was suggested by Star-Track software from Astrolabe. However, the weights I use are somewhat different.

7. Determining compatibility is one of the most common reasons for consulting an astrologer. Any competent astrologer should be able to give you a detailed reading of how well a relationship can work. The art of synastry--chart comparison--is far too complex to be reduced to a few element comparisons, but such comparisons are an important part of synastry. More to the point, they are quickly done and extremely helpful to the amateur. For a more detailed look at any specific relationship-- whether romantic, business, family, or friendship--check with a professional astrologer.

8. Again--and this is important--if this gets depressing or if you have emotional problems, see a therapist.

Chapter Appendix: Some Correspondences with the Elements

FIRE	EARTH	AIR	WATER

Chinese symbolism

FIRE	EARTH	AIR	WATER
yang	yin	yang	yin
		diamond	sapphire
ruby	gold	crystal	lapis lazuli
		silver	

Greco-Roman symbolism

FIRE	EARTH	AIR	WATER
masculine	feminine	masculine	feminine
salamander	gnome	sylph	undine
Mars	Venus	Jupiter	Neptune
summer	spring	winter	autumn
red	green	white	blue
blood	honey	water	milk
hot	cold	wet	dry
choleric	phlegmatic	melancholic	sanguine

Hindu symbolism

FIRE	EARTH	AIR	WATER
Ra	La	Ya	Va
vital heat	body	blood	breath
scepter/ lightning	lotus wheel	sword	bowl of blood

Judeo-Christian symbolism

FIRE	EARTH	AIR	WATER
lance	paten	sword	cup (Grail)
lion	bull	eagle	man
St. Mark	St. Luke	St. John	St. Matthew

FIRE	EARTH	AIR	WATER
Native American/Aztec symbolism			
flint	house	rabbit	sugar cane
tillage	magic	war	peace
south	east	north	west
*Occult and Mystical symbolism**			
active	receptive	active	receptive
intuitive	sensation	thinking	feeling
essential self	body	memories	spirit
passion	strength	communication	sensitivity
wands	pentacles	swords	cups
Aries	Taurus	Gemini	Cancer
Leo	Virgo	Libra	Scorpio
Sagittarius	Capricorn	Aquarius	Pisces
Crown	Mercy	Understanding	Wisdom
Severity	Splendor	Victory	Beauty
Foundation	Kingdom	Kingdom	Foundation

*Includes Jung's psychological types and the sephiroth of the Tree of Life.

Chapter 5

Karma:
Punishment or Preparation?

Character is fate.
--Heraclitus

Every man's life is a fairy tale written by God's fingers.
--Hans Christian Andersen

Almost everything conspicuously great is great in defiance:
has come into being in defiance of affliction and pain, poverty,
destitution, bodily weakness, vice, passion, and a thousand other
obstructions. . . . Forbearance in the fact of fate, beauty constant
under torture, are not merely passive. They are a positive
achievement, an explicit triumph.
--Thomas Mann, *Death in Venice*

Traditionally, two kinds of karma affect your life. Pralabd karma is
the karma you were born with; it shapes your current life and is traditionally considered the residue of previous lives. Kriyamen karma is the
kind you create in this life, which will shape your future life.[1] For the
purposes of this book, pralabd karma is simply called karma.

KARMA AS PUNISHMENT

The concept of karma is liable to a very serious abuse, one that many
deeply spiritual people avoid, but one that I have frequently encountered. Not everyone who defends this abusive attitude understands all the
motivations and problems inherent in it. They are laid bare here.

The traditional view of karma blames misfortunes--from birth defects to business failures--on the sins of previous lives. It was also used in India as a method of social control: because everyone was born into the caste he or she "deserved," it was easy to believe that the lower castes, including the Untouchables, were exploited and outcast only because they were spiritually inferior.[2]

Even today some people hold the opinion that the Ethiopians are starving because they are reincarnated Nazis suffering for having destroyed the Jews. But what karmic debt did the Jews and Gypsies and Poles and Lithuanians incur, that they had to die so horribly in the ovens of Dachau and Auschwitz? Why--if the victims were being punished for a karmic debt--did the Nazis have to suffer for killing them? They were only fulfilling their own law; no executioner is prosecuted for murder when he pulls the switch on the electric chair.

That attitude--what we might call karmic prejudice--actually creates a class of victims and a class of spiritually superior overlords. It encourages each to think of their respective fates as the unalterable will of God. It is the exact equivalent of the worn-out blame-the-victim mentality: she was asking to be raped, walking alone at night; she must have provoked him to hit her; if you were good, your parents wouldn't abuse and neglect you; he has AIDS because God is trying to punish homosexuals; if they'd behave, we wouldn't have to lynch them; if they had been civilized, we wouldn't have taken their land. They're poor, an ethnic minority, women, starving, sick, oppressed, raped, abused, conquered in this lifetime because they were naughty in a previous life.

Karmic Prejudice and the Privileged

Thinking that way may be comforting (or at least comfortable) for the privileged, those who do not so conspicuously suffer. The privileged feel no need to help the designated victims, whoever they may be, because they brought it on themselves and must now work out their karmic debt. The privileged are excused from helping other individuals and from trying to eradicate war, poverty, prejudice, and child abuse by changing society since the victims of these horrors brought it on themselves. Anyway, it's spiritual to suffer, and the karmically pure must not interfere with the destiny of the accursed.

The second reason is that the privileged person no longer needs to feel kinship with the miserable--no longer needs to wonder if those awful things couldn't happen to him- or herself. They brought it on themselves; I must be spiritually superior, because I haven't had those things happen--yet. Worse, the natural guilt-fed hatred the upper class feels toward the underclass is reinforced by wondering what the latter did in their previous lives to deserve such poverty, misery, and wretchedness. It's a splendid opportunity to despise the victims while self-righteously condemning them as reincarnated oppressors.

Nevertheless, few people manage to go through their lives without suffering at least a little--not even the wealthy, white, and privileged. This view of karma gives them no way to deal with the inevitable tragedies and losses. Knocked down from a comfortable position, never trained to deal with real suffering and pain, they cannot bring any trained spiritual insight to their situation.

Karmic Prejudice and the Victims

This view of karma is as bad for those defined as "victims" as it is for the privileged. Being lowly and accursed becomes a true self-definition, not an incidental condition that can be altered or at least made tolerable. The victim mentality is as destructive (not to mention unattractive) as is the Nietzschean superman mentality of the privileged. Yet, if the victim is being punished for past-life sins, all he or she can do is bear the dreadful pain and hope for an early death. This passivity is understandable but not very helpful.

A NEW VIEW OF KARMA

Not everyone who believes in traditional karmic reincarnation falls into this trap, and even those who do are usually unaware of the self-righteousness it causes. But it is a very serious problem. Is it really enlightened and spiritual to equate the social stratification of power and success with spiritual holiness--or is it a recycled version of the divine right of kings and the presidency above the law?

If you do believe in reincarnation, you can avoid the trap by keeping in mind that the next turn of the wheel may find you begging on the streets of Calcutta. If you don't believe in reincarnation, you can look on karma as I do: not as a punishment for past sins, but a preparation for future achievements. Christ's healing of a blind man addresses this problem directly. The disciples asked, "Who sinned, this man or his parents, that he should be born blind?" Jesus replied, "It was neither that this man sinned, nor his parents; but it was in order that the works of God might be displayed in him."[3]

Our karma--painful or easy--is not for punishment or reward, but to help us perform the works of God. Dealing with karma is not, therefore, accepting your fate because you're being punished; it's part of the pattern of your life, a pattern that has a meaningful and discoverable purpose.

On the way to discovering that purpose, the victim may have quite a difficult time. It's already too easy to think that any disaster is your own fault. The experience of a client of mine is a case in point.[4] Margaret, like most abused children, had learned to define herself as a victim: someone who deserves and will always attract disasters and pain. Believing that she was a worthless, loathsome, and contemptible creature who innately deserved the abuse, she made excuses for her abusive parents. Years of therapy helped her find emotional health by showing her that it was not, after all, her fault. Only after she was able to recognize that the problem had been not in her, but in her violent and unloving parents--to feel and accept her own rage at the abusers--could she forgive them, stop defining herself as a victim, find some self-esteem, and get on with her life. Imagine her feelings when she was told by a half-baked "new age" acquaintance that the abuse had, after all, been her own fault.

Margaret came to me feeling furiously angry and also unspiritual. What if it had been true? What if she had been punished for doing something awful in a previous life?

"The worst thing was the helplessness. I couldn't stop it. Now I'm told that I deserved it. If it's true, I'm going to start hating myself again. What can I do?"

Over weeks of work with me, Margaret began to understand the abuse not merely as a horrible and meaningless event that had scarred her permanently--an event she likened to being hit by a train. She became aware of the role that the abuse had played in shaping her life. It was an important part of her pattern, though not something she had deserved. She began to see that since she could never be rid of all the effects of abuse, she should use what she could of the experience. At my request, she listed what she had learned from the experience. Here is her list.

--I'm a survivor. If I could go through that, I can through anything.

--I think I'm more compassionate than I might have been. I can help and understand those who have suffered, and I'm even beginning to understand what drives the abusers. They've been hurt, too.

--I have learned about forgiving other people. That makes it easier to forgive myself, too!

--It helped me choose my job. [Margaret works to publicized the plight of the abused.]

--It made me depend on God. I know what I believe and I've tested it. If all that couldn't shake my faith, nothing can.

--The effects of abuse drove me to therapy and to other ways to try to understand myself. I've been forced to learn a lot about myself that I might not otherwise have known.

Viewing karma as a preparation for future achievements, rather than as a punishment for past sins, seems to be a much more constructive attitude. It helped Margaret reconcile the sense of purpose and design that her spiritual commitment gave her with the truths she had learned in psychotherapy. It can help those with much less severe problems as well.

In certain myths and fairy tales, the happy ending is only reached after the proper question is asked. The proper question about karma is not *What did I do to deserve this?* but *What am I supposed to learn from this?* When you stop worrying about being punished for past lives and begin to see karma as a kind of training, you can start to fulfill your destiny in life.

DISCOVERING YOUR KARMA

The following exercises are designed to help you understand how the circumstances of your life work into the pattern--the pattern you have already begun to perceive. In order to see your karma clearly, you must be absolutely honest. That is painful; you may be able to do it only in stages. Just tell the truth as you see it when you're working; later it may be changed by remembering or understanding other incidents or factors. If you have had a particularly difficult life, or if you find yourself getting depressed, you may want to talk about some of these issues with a trained, professional therapist.

1. Are You Resolving It or Repeating It?

Certain situations come up over and over again in our lives. Psychologists know this as the repetition of a trauma; to a metaphysician, it also has karmic significance. If you don't resolve the central conflict, you must repeat it. These exercises will help you identify some of the recurring themes in your life.

Crystal Exercise

Choose three stones from a balanced group of stones and crystals (the set of interpretations uses the set from *The Crystal Tree*). The first represents the nature of your karma, the second your hidden feelings about it, the third the training it is giving you. For interpretations, see Table 5.1.

Stone 1 _____

Stone 2 _____

Stone 3 _____

Visualizing

Visualize yourself stuck in a situation that has endlessly repeated itself in your life--conflict with a parent or in-law, a dead-end relationship, a self-destructive act, whatever. Imagine yourself resolving it instead of repeating it. Try different solutions in your visualization. Dream it through several times. Write down the best three solutions in your journal. How have you dealt with it in the past? Which tactics helped and which hurt? How would the situation change if you dealt with it differently?

Journal Exercise

Write about a repetitive situation. When was the first time it happened? Does it remind you of anything in your family history? How do you get past the block when it occurs? What is the benefit to not resolving it?

Why are you afraid to let it go?

Try playing a different role in the situation. Pretend you are an innocent bystander and describe, as objectively as you can, what happens in the situation. Pretend you are your opponent or another person in the situation and look at it from their viewpoint. What is their payback for acting as they do? How do they frame the experience? That is, what significance does it have for them? In what context do they see you and the situation? Why are they participating in it?

Art Exercise

Draw (or otherwise express) your central conflict. What does it look like?

2. Can You Forgive?

Forgiveness is necessary but difficult. Edith Cavell, about to be executed by the Germans for smuggling refugees out of the country, said, "I must have no anger or bitterness toward anyone." Holding onto rage and pain instead of forgiving is crippling. Yet forgiving isn't easy; it entails acknowledging that you have been hurt (and are therefore vulnerable) as well as accepting that you, too, can hurt people (a hard admission to make, and part of dealing with the Shadow). It also entails understanding another person's motivations.

All the understanding, all the compassion in the world, will not help unless you seize your own power and let go of the pain. Until you forgive those who have hurt you, you are still in their power. Your feelings are still controlled by their actions.

These exercises are designed to help you work through some of the pain and anger of your hurts, and then to help you forgive.

Visualizing

Imagine yourself forgiving your worst enemy and asking forgiveness from someone you've harmed. Then do it!

Journal Exercise

What can't you forgive? Why? Write a letter to the person you cannot forgive, explaining what he or she has done to hurt you and how the hurt can be healed. (You don't have to send the letter, but you might consider doing so.) You might write a series of letters; the early ones would work through the pain, and the later ones might express some understanding of why the person acted as he or she did. In that way you may find the strength to forgive.

Music Exercise

Listen to healing music. Repeat forgiveness to yourself.

3. What Is the Destiny of Karma?

The link between destiny and karma has already been shown, but you still must see for yourself the patterns of your life. These exercises are designed to help you see the pattern clearly.

Crystal Exercise

Choose three stones from a balanced group of stones and crystals. The first represents the purpose of your karma, the second your hidden feelings about it, the third the training it is giving you. For interpretations, see Table 5.1.

Stone 1 _____

Stone 2 _____

Stone 3 _____

Visualizing

Imagine the pattern of your life. What structure does it have? How is karma guiding you?

Journal Exercise

Write down your karma. What is it teaching you? Try to make sense of the disconnected events of your life. Assuming there is an intelligence guiding your learning process, where does it seem to be going? List the things unhappiness has taught you. List the things happiness has taught you.

Art Exercise

Draw, sculpt, dance, or otherwise express the pattern of your karma.

Game-Playing

Play Smoke with your karma.

NOTES

1. Stephen Arroyo, *Astrology, Karma and Transformation* (Davis, Calif.: CRCS, 1975), p. 6.

2. *The Larousse Encyclopedia of Mythology* (New York: Hamlyn, 1959), p. 326.

3. John, chapter 9. The whole chapter is devoted to this remarkable healing and the reactions of those who would not believe it.

4. All case histories are from my own practice; clients' names and identifying details have been changed in order to protect their privacy. Some case histories may be composites.

Table 5.1: Crystals and Their Meanings

The crystal set consists of rose quartz, red cullet, red jasper, carnelian, cat's eye (known sometimes as tiger's eye), brown agate, aventurine, green quartz, hematite, sodalite, chevron amethyst, amethyst, clear crystal, half-clear crystal, silent stone (snow quartz), Montana agate, smoky quartz, and onyx.

Rose Quartz

Physical: Friendship, intimacy, closeness.
Psychological: Harmony and affection, close family ties, the need for love and approval.
Spiritual: Surrender to God.
Shadow: Giving in, lack of self-assertion, going along with the crowd.

Red Cullet

Physical: Individualism, passion, and sexuality.
Psychological: Passion, creation, art. Independence and rebellion.
Spiritual: Spiritual transformation and renewal, the spirit of seeking.
Shadow: Jealousy, self-centeredness.

Red Jasper

Physical: Restlessness, change, curiosity.
Psychological: Spirit of seeking, self-examination, analysis.
Spiritual: The spirit of the quest, of the pilgrim.
Shadow: Change for its own sake--or the refusal to change and grow.

Carnelian

Physical: Warm and affectionate friendships, parties, and celebrations.
Psychological: Emotional ties based on knowledge of the other person, not on mystery and uncertainty. The need to understand and analyze relationships.
Spiritual: Reverence for life. The attitude that pleasure is of God and is therefore holy. Mystical union with God and all creation.

Shadow: Manipulativeness, lack of self-respect, overindulgence, hiding behind a social group.

Cat's Eye

Physical: Insight, shrewdness, vision.
Psychological: The gift of understanding others' problems. Often the mark of someone who is dedicated to helping others.
Spiritual: Willingness to forgive, understanding the flaws of yourself and others.
Shadow: Judgmental spirit, cattiness, gossip.

Brown Agate

Physical: Caution and good judgment. Slow and careful preparation.
Psychological: Self-discipline.
Spiritual: Penance, justice, scrupulous fairness.
Shadow: Pessimism; gloom; worry, often over petty matters. Insecurity and fear.

Green Quartz

Physical: Strength of character, self-esteem.
Psychological: Blending the unconscious with the conscious. Willingness to face your own dark side. The ability to interpret dreams.
Spiritual: The Kingdom of God within you.
Shadow: Nightmares, phobias, emotional problems. The separation of spiritual and physical life.

Aventurine

Physical: Great physical enjoyment, health, taking pleasure in the body.
Psychological: Balance between body, soul, and spirit. A healthy and innocent enjoyment of physical pleasures.
Spiritual: Freely offering of the body to God.
Shadow: Physical illness, stress, and separation from (or too much absorption in) the body.

Hematite

Physical: Enduring love, desire controlled by idealism, complete commitment.
Psychological: The discipline to transform dreams into reality. Sustained commitment to a dream.
Spiritual: Continuing devotion to God despite adverse circumstances.
Shadow: Rigidity, fault-finding. Inability to make a commitment or stick to a project.

Sodalite

Physical: Achievement, success, hard work rewarded.
Psychological: Getting your just desserts--knowing what you deserve and asking for it.
Spiritual: Freedom from greed, taking no thought for tomorrow.
Shadow: Materialism, greed, lack of compassion.

Chevron Amethyst

Physical: Organization, structure, neatness.
Psychological: The final integration of the personality.
Spiritual: The order of heaven.
Shadow: Snobbishness, wrong priorities, inhuman bureaucracy.

Amethyst

Physical: Psychic talents combined with common sense. Great success.
Psychological: Psychic powers used well, self-knowledge and self-control.
Spiritual: A true spirit. Proper values.
Shadow: Using psychic knowledge for destructive purposes (very dangerous).

Crystal (clear)

Physical: Psychic abilities and clarity of outlook. Emotional harmony and peace.

Psychological: The integrated personality. Good relationships with others based on self-respect.
Spiritual: Clear views of spiritual truth.
Shadow: Arrogance, fear of change.

Crystal (half-clear)

Physical: Confusion, hasty or prejudiced thinking. Not letting yourself see the whole situation.
Psychological: Hiding the truth from yourself (usually to protect someone else).
Spiritual: The beginning of wisdom: knowing that you don't know.
Shadow: Refusing to trust yourself.

Silent Stone (snow quartz)

Physical: New beginnings and ideas.
Psychological: Waiting for the right time to make new beginnings.
Spiritual: The start of a new way of thinking. Protecting new ideas from hostile people.
Shadow: Being overly cautious or overly eager.

Montana Agate

Physical: Memories and persons from the past turn up. Opportunities to correct past mistakes.
Psychological: Unconscious worries or influences from the past.
Spiritual: Recalling past problems in order to avoid them in the future.
Shadow: Restraint, fear, lack of forgiveness of yourself and others.

Smoky Quartz

Physical: The ability or need to conceal yourself from other people. A dramatic temperament.
Psychological: Hiding your true self in order to be liked or accepted. Adaptability.
Spiritual: Struggling to find a true path. The faith is there, but the way is not evident.

Shadow: Self-blame, hypersensitivity.

Onyx

Physical: Strength, courage, endurance.
Psychological: Getting to the root of the problem--a painful but necessary process.
Spiritual: Rebirth after a period of suffering and dryness.
Shadow: Giving up; refusing to enjoy anything for fear it will be taken away.

Chapter 6

Creativity and Renewal: Awakening Your Senses

The clearest way into the Universe is through a forest wilderness.

--John Muir, *John of the Mountains*

Speak to the earth, and it will teach thee.
--Job 12:8

There is a pleasure in the pathless woods,
There is a rapture on the lonely shore,
There is a society where none intrudes,
By the deep sea, and music in its roar,
I love not man the less, but nature more,
From these our interviews, in which I steal
From all I may be, or have been before,
To mingle with the Universe, and feel
What I can ne'er express, yet cannot all conceal.
--Lord Byron, *Childe Harold's Pilgrimage*

Ordinary life--when it is perceived as ordinary--can dull the senses as use dulls knives. But a good knife, properly used, may never grow dull. The following exercises will help you reawaken your senses and relearn the joys of living creatively. Visualization can help you become more aware of your senses and the world around you; the same technique serves to refresh your spirit, providing a free mini-vacation. The key to creative living is awareness: awareness of the joy available to all, awareness of the spiritual dimensions of life, awareness of the miraculous natural world.

RAISING AWARENESS WITH VISUALIZATION

Visualization is most often used as a tool for self-improvement. You visualize the changes you want to make, imagining how you will look when you have lost 20 pounds or what you will do when you have the new job. Then you imagine every step of the new exercise program or the job interview. When you visualize yourself overcoming potential problems, you give yourself more courage and more skill to meet the challenges. What you imagine becomes real. You have already encountered the technique half a dozen times in this book.

However, there is another use for visualization, one that is less goal-directed. You might recognize it from childhood; you may even have been punished for doing it. But daydreaming is important. It can be a lifesaver. It is necessary--unquestionably so--for artists, writers, and other creative people. It is equally necessary for anyone who wants to live creatively. Daydreaming can give you rest when you are weary. When you cannot afford to spend six months and ten thousand dollars on a voyage to the South Seas, you can afford a daydream.

The Sensuous Image and the Audiovisual Daydream

Sometimes you simply need a break from everyday stress, a short exercise in creativity. Then you can concentrate on a single image. Trying to imagine it whole is part of the challenge. A truly sensuous image has all the impact of seeing the real thing for the first time.

Permit me a brief digression into definitions. Despite all the sex books of the 1970s, *sensuous* does not mean *sexual* or even *sensual*. It applies specifically to images, poetic or otherwise, that have the force, vividness, and weight of reality, that offer not just an abstract idea but a concrete, rounded, and complete experience of the senses--tactile, olfactory, and so on. "J" should have been the sensual woman (interested in carnal pleasures) rather than the sensuous woman (an image evoking a response from the senses). That delicate distinction is being lost, but it is worth preserving. Your daydreams do not have to be about sex to be sensuous, though careful attention to all the senses is likely to improve your sex life immeasurably.

Why bother evoking scent and texture? Isn't a standard audiovisual daydream enough?

No. It is not enough for the simple and unarguable reason that it does not work as well. A daydream limited to sound and sight is like a television show. It will serve to pass the time, but it rarely has power to nourish the spirit. Worse, what you might think of as an ordinary daydream is probably couched in abstracts, which are useful and can be mind-expanding, but not when you use them as shorthand. An abstract image must be thought out, felt as thoroughly as any concrete image, for it to take hold of your mind and heart. It cannot seize you on its own.

Art is the ultimate daydream, the ultimate renewal of self. (It is also a challenge and a guide, but here we are dealing only with its ability to transport us to other times and places, to make us see into others' hearts.) Art refreshes because it takes you elsewhere. Great literature, great music, great art, all have that quality of immersing you in another world. Through ink on paper, books convey the scent of lilacs or the taste of madeleines dipped in tea. The painted apples of Cézanne are redolent of cider on a fall afternoon, and Monet's water lilies have the drowsy scent of still lakes in the sun. Everyone who listens to Beethoven's Ode to Joy dances--dances in the heart, and the breath and the pulse run faster.

If you will let your creative inner fires free, if you will daydream with heart and mind and flesh, so that you can taste, smell, feel, and touch as well as see and hear, you can give yourself the refreshment that true art gives. You may even tap into a well of talent that, with hard work and dedication and increasing skill, may give that same renewal to others, and so transform yourself into an artist.

The Enemy

What is the enemy of creativity? It is prepackaged life--all the things that you use and do and feel without ever examining them to see if they truly belong to you. It is assuming that other people are wooden figures instead of humans, that your neighbor is an *it* rather than a *thou*. It is seeing yourself as an it. It is letting others' assumptions about what you should like and want and value become a substitute for your own inner knowledge of your needs. It is welcoming mediocrity (another name for cowardice) because "It's not exciting, but it doesn't hurt much." It is the deliberate dulling of your senses; flattening of feelings; rejection of yourself in favor of status, acceptance, or whatever other false gods tempt you. It is laziness daily weakening you. It is crawling miserably in and out of a place to live instead of leaving home for adventures and returning for joy and sharing.

Sometimes it is despair, sickness, loneliness, the scars of dreadful pain. But all those things can be overcome, if you dare, if you let yourself take the risk of learning to love and live instead of existing.

Sometimes the enemy is no more and no worse than mere habit. Modern technology has provided us with a video hypnotist that effectively destroys creativity and leaves us with nothing. Television makes us passive and receptive; it effectively conveys only certain kinds of information; it allows no response (you can always scribble in the margins of a book, or write the author a letter, or--if the author is dead-- write an essay on the author's errors). Vision has been condensed to what we see on a television screen. Remember that a television screen--like a window screen--filters selectively as well as projects an image. All too often, when you try to daydream, the television image seems to be what is real and desirable. Television is only sound and sight--the sound of laughtracks, the sight of improbably perfect and wealthy and handsome actors.

An evening of watching television rarely gives you real renewal. It is too slight a form to pack much emotional wallop--with rare and brilliant exceptions, it does not go to the heart of any matter. Its laughs are canned and savorless; its tears are wrung from the eyes and not the heart. Real renewal is based on real, felt emotion--genuine, with no tricks, no tired formulas, based on what you truly feel and desire and enjoy.

Awareness and Daydreams

Making the effort to daydream fully is unexpectedly rewarding. Your visualizations will gain new power and immediacy. You will return deeply refreshed by even the briefest daydream. You will find yourself noticing the taste and texture of daily life with far more appreciation. Can you really afford to pass up a new source of true pleasure? Being aware is not immoral, illegal, or fattening. At first it takes some effort, for truly you must be trained to joy. Images can help you find an inner stillness and sense of peace.

The reason sensuous awareness works is that we were designed to be creatures of all our senses. Exercise your senses--with daydreams and in your ordinary life. Here are some sample escapes. Sit back, close your eyes, and imagine one of these places or things. (Don't try them all at once, or you will exhaust yourself.) You may feel foolish at first, but relax and let it flow. No one will judge you. Don't be discouraged if you have a hard time concentrating at first; you will improve with practice.

Think of Africa, the Serengeti, the broad plains with their short thick grass cropped by zebra. The sun is heavy here, a weight on the back of the neck. Strange insects sing in the thorn bushes. The short trampled grass is aromatic in the sun; it smells scorched and hot. In the midday stillness, the wild creatures rest. Their pungent smell and the thick smell of blood still hang over the plain, shimmering in the heat. Under the rough soft fur, the lions are muscled with iron.

Think of sailing ships made of wood, canvas, rope; entirely natural and yet made by the hand of man, the only machine that rivals wild things in beauty. Plunging through ocean swells, the motion of the ship is also a sound: creaking timbers, wind sighing through the rigging, the soft sound of sails, the clink of chains, the slap and rush of the waves. Salt-soaked wood is aromatic in the sun, redolent of seaweed and old voyages. The brass rail is polished, smooth, cool in the shade and almost hot in the light.

In winter, think of the tender rush of early spring, of white and pale and dark lilacs, fragrant, full-leaved, with the rain lying in the stiff-cupped flowers. Even the dark branches are aromatic. The fine rain has ended; the warm breeze shakes droplets of water on you as you walk. The rustling leaves and clicking branches have a soft hypnotic sound, inextricable from the fragrance of lilac. The ground--frozen so long-- yields a little under your feet; it has the pleasantly musty smell of wet earth. Drifting clouds unveil the late-afternoon sun; suddenly light pours over you, making tiny rainbows of the last droplets on the leaves.

In summer, think of the gypsyish stirrings of blood in autumn, the bright leaves and smoky air. Eager and restless, you walk through night and rising wind, feeling in the stretch of your muscles the satisfaction of your restless mind. In this uneasy season you could walk forever. All day the sun shone on glowing leaves; in late afternoon, leaf-fires burned, their sweet smoke thickening the air. Now at night the wind is stirring the carefully raked piles, and you kick your way through unraked leaves, hearing the satisfying rustle even louder in the dark.

Having walked (in the spring rain, the autumn wind), you are home again. A little chilled, a little aching--it's been ages since you walked that far!--you look forward to making a hot cup of tea. In the bright kitchen, you notice again your own belongings. Earlier they had been almost invisible, just a random clutter. Refreshed by your walk, you see them again with loving eyes. The copper bowl shines not just with polish but with memories of buying it together at a flea market, when you were first in love. The calendar towel reminds you of Great Grandma, whose kitchen was always festooned with calendar towels for the previous twenty years or so; maybe that's why you bought so unfashionable a thing. The plain tea kettle that's whistling now--that was the first thing you bought for your first apartment; its whistle and jet of steam were signals of independence. The steaming tea, poured into the mug you had in college, tastes comforting, thoroughly domestic, with just a hint of the woody smokiness of autumn.

The first two visualizations were impersonal--you imagined a place and a thing. The next three were personal--you imagined yourself in different seasons or in your kitchen. The first two required effort to imagine something you may never have seen, but you may have found it easier to be aware of all sensory cues in such unusual situations. The three "realistic" visualizations required you only to recall the taste, touch, and smell of familiar things. Both exercises made you aware of the gestalt: everything going on around you.

Let's take visualization a step further. In imagining the sailing ship and the plains of the Serengeti, you were an invisible and intangible observer. In the next exercises, you will imagine yourself in truly impossible situations, beginning with the most similar (the lion of the Serengeti) and moving progressively toward the least similar (the living rock). This exercise will help you stretch your imagination and make yourself aware of lives unlike your own; in doing so, you will increase your sensitivity to both your own life and the lives of dissimilar creatures. As the visualized self grows less and less human, I have given increasingly complete questions to help guide you. The lion is very like ourselves; the ship is familiar because we make and name and control ships; the hurricane can be directly experienced, though it is unlike us in scale, speed, thought; the bedrock can be seen and touched but is in almost all other ways on no human scale because it is huge, ancient, immobile.

If you prefer, you may do your visualization first, without reading my clues. Then you can check with my questions, see what elements you may have missed, and return to your vision.

As usual, after the visualizations, you may want to record one or all of them in your notebook. Some questions afterward will help you clarify your thinking about your visions. You may find yourself turning to these again and again, seeking a glimpse of peace in the rock or power in the lion. They can calm and soothe, help send you to sleep on insomniac nights, and refresh you on dreary bus rides. Don't ever try them as you drive or operate machinery, and I wouldn't recommend doing visualization on the subway, either--you might get mugged.

Visualize yourself as a lion of the Serengeti. Feel your lion body: muscular, golden, graceful. Feel your lion senses: What do you taste and smell? What do you see and hear? How does it feel to move and stretch and play as a lion? How does your mind think? What do you want? How do you respond to the slow turning of the seasons, to the swifter change between night and morning? How do you feel about aging? Are you a lion or a lioness?

Think of yourself as the ship on the ocean. Feel the wholeness of you: high masts, taut sails, slim prow joyfully cleaving the water. What are you most aware of? Can you sense the shifts of the wind? Are you frightened, exhilarated, timid, eager, plodding, swift? Do you respond to the hand on your ship's wheel, or do you rebel a little? Can you sense what lies under the waves? How far down? Do the gulls and seabirds annoy or amuse you? Do you like sailing, or do you miss being in port? Does the solitude bother you? How do you feel about your crew? Do you remember having been a tree? Does it seem strange to have grown tall and sturdy and immobile, feeling movement as the wind in your branches, and now to be a creature running before the wind?

Let yourself become a hurricane. Feel yourself rising, funnelling wind, moving over seas and lands. What are you most aware of? Can you sense the difference between yourself and the calmer airs? Do you see and feel the seas below you or the lands you cross? Are you aware of your part in the natural order, or do you feel lawless? Do you like yourself?

Are you happy, sad, dutiful, exuberant, resigned? Are you aware that you are remaking landscapes? How does it make you feel? What do you want? Are you sorry when you dissolve into a tropical storm and then into the greater atmosphere? Is that death to you, or is being a hurricane only a single episode in a long and pleasurable life as a wind? Do you have a sense of accomplishment? How do you sense the tides, the motion of the Earth beneath you? Do you ever get tired and want to stay in one place?

Imagine yourself as a geological formation: not just a rock, but a layer of rock between other layers of rock. Huge, weighty, and still, you are stretched under thousands of acres of land. At road cuts and a few other places, you show an edge of yourself in an outcrop. What are you like? Are you buried deeply or near the surface? What can you sense of the heat of the molten core beneath you, of the weight of the grass and people and soil above you? What kind of rock are you: sedimentary (made from sediment deposited at the bottom of streams or seas, like limestone), igneous (made from cooling magma--liquid rock--like granite), or metamorphic (transformed from a sedimentary or igneous rock by great heat or pressure, like marble)? What specific rock are you? What color? Has any of you ever been quarried, and did it hurt? Do you communicate with your lost, chipped-off stones? How do you communicate with other rock formations? What is the landscape like over you? (You help shape it, you know.) If you underlie hills and valleys, were you bent and folded to make them, or did streams cut through you to make the valleys? Are there farms, suburbs, cities, or perhaps wilderness lying over you? Can you sense the creatures--unimaginable, almost, to you-- that, tiny and quick as insects, skitter over the top of the world? Do you sense day and night, the seasons and the years, or do you measure time by the movement of the galaxy? You are millions of years old; how do you sense time?

Which visualization did you like best? _____

Why? _____

_____

_____

Which did you like least? _____

Why? _____

_____

_____

What qualities in the lion's life did you most enjoy? _____

_____

_____

_____

Why? _____

_____

_____

What qualities in the lion's life did you least enjoy? _____

_____

_____

_____

Why? _____

_____

_____

What qualities in the ship's life did you most enjoy? _____

_____

_____

_____

Why? _____

_____

_____

What qualities in the ship's life did you least enjoy? _____

_____

_____

_____

Why?_____

_____

_____

What qualities in the hurricane's life did you most enjoy? _____

_____

_____

_____

Why? _____

_____

_____

What qualities in the hurricane's life did you least enjoy? _____

_____

_____

_____

Why? _____

_____

_____

What qualities in the rock's life did you most enjoy? _____

_____

_____

_____

Why? _____

_____

_____

What qualities in the rock's life did you least enjoy? _____

_____

_____

_____

Why? _____

_____

_____

List three qualities from the lion's life that you would like to incorporate into your own life. _____

_____

_____

List some ways you can do so. _____

_____

_____

_____

_____

_____

List three qualities from the ship's life that you would like to incorporate into your own life. _____

_____

_____

_____

List some ways you can do so. _____

_____

_____

_____

_____

List three qualities from the hurricane's life that you would like to incorporate into your own life. _____

_____

_____

List some ways you can do so. _____

_____

_____

_____

_____

_____

List three qualities from the rock's life that you would like to incorporate into your own life. _____

_____

_____

_____

List some ways you can do so. _____

_____

_____

_____

_____

_____

LIVING IN HARMONY WITH THE EARTH

Now you have been a lion, a ship, a storm, a rock. Do you feel refreshed and alive? You may have added the lion's keen senses or the ship's joy in motion to your awareness; you may have felt your own power in the power of the storm or your own endurance in the ancient rock. Those qualities are yours now, though you may not have been aware of them before or connected what you felt with the worlds of other creatures. The complete imagining, almost being, of totally different creatures (if I may so call them) can also help you live in better harmony with the Earth. When you have been a storm or a rock, you will have more understanding and respect for the planet, which is, after all, a rock wrapped in storms.

We were designed to live in harmony with the Earth. Despite cars, central heating, electric light, and food that comes wrapped in plastic from the store instead of in its own integrity from the earth or the sea, we can still do so. I do not ask you to leave your home for the Alaskan wilderness or to begin spinning your own flax to make your own clothing. There are benefits to buying clothing (or at least cloth) ready-made, to having our houses heated in winter and air-conditioned in summer, even to frozen dinners destined to be microwaved for five minutes at full power (turn 90 degrees after the first two-and-a-half minutes). But the price, all too often, is that we lose the sense of seasons and time, that we grow accustomed to tasteless food and sterile smells. There is little or no connection between what we eat and wear and what we do to earn our food and clothes. We have lost the sense of process, and with it, most of our senses.

That sense of process can be regained.

If you live in the country, it is easier to see the connections than it is for those who live in the city, simply because in the country the natural world is not yet dominated by people. The stars shine at night, instead of being washed out by the glare of streetlights, and you can see the slow change from the winter stars to the summer stars. Weather is not something mentioned on the radio, but a living reality when you can watch cloud shadows chasing over the hills. Because the effects of drought or untimely rain are seen and felt, you become naturally aware of wind, rain, and weather. The seasons are not merely signals to get out or put away lighter or heavier clothing (not that it really matters, because the indoor temperature is the same, summer or winter); the daily work is premised on the seasons.

In the country it is self-evident that milk comes not from a square waxen box decorated with the faces of missing children, but from cows who eat hay nourished by sunlight and rain and who cannot give milk until they have borne a calf. You see what the milk is for and where it is from, and you can taste it unprocessed with the cream thick in the top. When the cows come into the barn for the winter, they change their diet, and you can taste that change in the milk.

All these factors--the closeness to the earth, the importance of the seasons, the awareness of the process--give country people an unquestioned affinity with nature. Is there hope, though, for those of us who (like me at this stage of my life) choose to live or are forced to live in urban areas?

Of course. City life need not dull the senses and the sympathies; the city-dweller just has to put more effort and more awareness into what comes readily to the country person. The exercises here can help make the city dweller aware of the natural world. These are not quick exercises; they take time, because the Earth is slow. However, they can give you a sense of process.

EXERCISES

Every day, in your journal, write down what the weather is like. Describe the look of the sky and the feel of the wind, as well as temperature and humidity. Look at the daily paper or in an almanac for the length of the day as well. As you continue to keep the weather diary, note that you become more aware of the natural world. You should even begin to be able to predict the weather in your area; close observation of the sky and the wind beats the National Weather Service every time.

Get up early to watch the dawn. In that uncontaminated solitude and space, there is peace and a new awareness of the natural order of things.

Get a field guide to flowers, trees, insects, birds, or minerals. Take nature walks (in your local park or nature center) to identify the plants, animals, and stones you see every day and never notice.

Celebrate the seasons. Become aware of the spring and autumn equinoxes and the winter and summer solstices. Many religious holidays are tied to these dates, as well as to the midpoints. The winter solstice is near Christmas, Hanukkah, and Kwaanza. The spring equinox is marked by Easter and Passover. The summer solstice has the confusingly named Midsummer Day (also called St. John's Day), when celebrants leap over fires. At the autumn equinox is the Jewish New Year. The midpoints (February 2, May 1, August 1, and October 31) are also holidays, though not as generally celebrated. They are Candlemas (Feast of the Purification of Our Lady), May Day (another festival for Mary), Lammas (a harvest festival), and of course Halloween (followed by All Saints and All Souls).

In each season, depending on where you live, there will be typical moods, weathers, lengths of day, activities. Enjoy these. Do the things the season asks for, whether that is making angels in the snow or cutting tulips and daffodils. Obviously, some places have more or less highly differentiated seasons. Arctic Alaska has winters that mean business, while a Hawaiian winter offers little scope for making snow angels. I'm not telling you to conform to the kind of upstate Pennsylvania year I am used to, with a long cold winter, slow late spring, two weeks of warm summer, and sparkling magnificent autumn. I'm telling you to notice the one where you live--whether you live in Australia, where August is the depth of winter, or in Hawaii, Maine, or San Francisco.

Plant a seed or a cutting outdoors or in a pot on your windowsill and tend it until it is a grown plant. Easy plants to grow include coleus (from seed or cutting), philodendron, pothos, Swedish ivy (all from cuttings), marigolds (from seed). Many herbs can also be easily grown indoors or out. Even a carrot top can be rooted in water; it grows lovely, lacy foliage.

Visit a working farm and spend some time getting the feeling of growing things. If you are close to a working colonial farm or to Amish or Mennonite communities, visit these to discover how food is grown without the intervention of chemicals, machinery, and the internal combustion engine. At least some of your ancestors probably lived and worked this way on farms.

Read about geology. It will give you a sense of the massive continuity of the Earth, the unimaginable stretches of time needed to create a world. Look at rock outcrops wherever you find them--and they are everywhere. If you can make a trip to a cave, go underground and feel the depth and strength of the Earth.

Learn a little astronomy. Get a star map and learn to identify the constellations. Even in cities you can usually see the Big Dipper. You can also go out to darker country areas to look at the sky. Notice the changes between the winter sky and the summer sky. On a mild night, lie out in a dark country place and look at the stars. On a clear night you can see not only the usual constellations but also the Milky Way. The stars on such nights are not white spangles against a flat sky. They are flaming, multicolored points hanging in three-dimensional space; you can see the depths and the distances, not just a flat arch. Check your almanac for the dates of meteor showers; few sights match the Perseid meteor shower on a clear, hot August night.

Chapter 7

Divination:
A Map Through the Maze

Poor intricated soul! Riddling, perplexed, labyrinthical soul!
--John Donne, *Sermons* (25 January 1628/1629)

. . . leave all meaner things
To low ambition, and the pride of kings.
Let us (since life can little more supply
Than just to look about us and to die)
Expatiate free o'er all this scene of man;
A mighty maze! but not without a plan.
--Alexander Pope, *Essay on Man*

This chapter deals with divination, not just as a professional activity, but as a personal one, like looking in a mirror. That mirror is the Tarot: not the only mirror by any means, but a very useful one. You will learn how to look at the symbols of the Tarot and see the forces that shape your inner self. The Tarot taught here is less predictive than symbolic, less concerned with whether you will find true love than whether you will find true peace. Predictive divination is not neglected. It can be a powerful tool when appropriately used. But appropriate use is not usually discussed in how-to texts. Covered here is when, where, and why divination should be used. I have also included a section on professional psychics and fortune tellers and how to choose a good one and how to identify and deal with a fraud or an incompetent reader.

Most of the many books that teach how to do divination discuss technique without ever mentioning the reasons for using the technique, but this chapter will deal with when divination is and is not appropriate.

(For those interested in learning to do divination for others, the list of further references at the back of the book includes books on how to tell fortunes for others using Tarot cards, crystals, and other techniques.) But first a deeper look into the art of divination. What is divination and how does it work?

THE MEANING AND USES OF DIVINATION

Divination is a kind of guided meditation focusing on a specific act: the understanding of where you are now and where you are going. It calls, not on outward forces, but on your deepest self. Though it is not an essential step to finding the inner grail, divination can be a powerful tool for self-discovery if it is used properly.

Divination can tell you nothing you do not already know. Because your own deepest knowledge is sometimes hidden from you, you may need the Tarot (or other techniques) to act as a mirror to help you discover what you already know. You may even need the help of a professional psychic to uncover the most deeply buried knowledge.

How Divination Works

But how do readings work? How can a stranger look at some brightly colored cards and tell you what will occur or what archetypal forces are influencing you? The essential principle of all metaphysics is "as above, so below." These four cryptic words express the great truth that everything in the Universe reflects everything else; the lesser reflects the form of the greater, as the shape of the solar system is echoed in the shape of the atom. If you know how and where to look, you can begin to understand how all of creation sings together. Your life is part of that song.

Specifically, anyone doing divination taps into the collective unconscious. Perhaps a metaphor can best explain how this works. Think of the collective unconscious as an aquifer, an underground sea of shared ideas and thoughts that links us all. Every individual has a well that sinks into that aquifer. A psychic has developed the ability to swim through the night sea and find what is clogging, poisoning, or otherwise influencing a person's water supply. Thus specific thoughts and bits of information (which are stored above the aquifer) rarely come through; strong emotions, deep archetypal influences, and the traces of important events are readily accessible. The skilled psychic can interpret the chaotic flood of emotion. Making sense of feelings of abandonment, for example, may require the psychic to distinguish between the primal early childhood fear, the history of actual losses, and the dreaded coming abandonment. It is a delicate, demanding task and can be extremely exhausting both physically and emotionally.

Divination and the Grail Quest

Most people think of divination as a strictly predictive tool: Will I get a new job, find true love, and raise healthy children? But the predictive aspect (which is discussed at length in a following section) is not the most important use of divination.

The role divination plays in the grail search is not predictive but symbolic. The cards of the major arcana symbolize archetypes--basic forces and ideas that shape your psyche. The cards act almost as a medieval version of the Rorschach test. How you choose, combine, and interpret the symbols of the major arcana can help you recognize the deep influences on your life and how you tend to react to them.

Prediction, Free Will, and Fate

Prediction raises certain questions that do bear on the purpose and meaning of the quest. How much of life is predestined? If something is foreseen, must it occur? Can you change the future? Can you change the past?

The future is not a set of railroad tracks. You are not limited to the choice of going forward to a specific destiny or derailing. Yet certain things in life seems predestined; there are places where you have to come, people you must confront. Again, a metaphor is the only way to express this truth. The future is like a maze. You can, through predictive readings, get an idea of the choices ahead of you and of some of their ramifications. In that sense you get a map through the maze (or at least the next section of it).

But the choices, the possible turnings, can give you a sense of what to avoid as well as what to seek out.

For example, if an illness, an accident, or a new job is foreseen, it does not *have* to come to pass. You may, through care of your health, prevent the illness or turn it into something minor. Caution may help you avert an accident. Laziness may keep you from getting a job. Just because it shows up in the reading doesn't mean you will get it. You still have to show up at the job interview, and your actions still influence whether you get it or not.

Or, to change the metaphor, a predictive reading is like a weather report (though usually somewhat more accurate). The weather report tells you about prevailing conditions and influences. You still have the choice whether or not to wear your raincoat or drive in an ice storm.

In other words, you do have free will, but your free will, combined with the pattern of your karma, will bring you again and again into places where you must make a choice. The choice then determines what choices will come next. To illustrate: You cannot choose today to have sex and tomorrow choose to be a virgin. You have made that choice impossible. You can choose to be celibate, but that is not the same thing.

When and Why to Get a Reading

Readings may help you make an intelligent choice, but (especially if you go to a professional psychic), you should never expect the reading or the reader to make the choice for you. Far too many people give away their power and their freedom by giving others the right to choose for them. Choose for yourself. Get advice or counsel from your mate, your friends, your family, your clergyperson, but choose for yourself.

Times of choice are not the only times for a reading. The following list gives some ideas of when you may want a reading.

--When you are confused and in need of clarification about a specific situation.

--When you are beginning a new year (either at your birthday or in January or at the spring or fall equinox: whenever you celebrate the beginning of a new year).

--When you have chosen or begun a new project, a new way of life, a new path.

--When you have ended or decided to end an old project, an old way of life, an old path.

--During important astrological transits: the Saturn returns, for example, which occur when you are about 29 and 58. (Check with your astrologer for specific dates.)

FORMS OF DIVINATION

In this chapter, due to space limitations, we are looking only at the Tarot. It is highly symbolic and meaningful, it can easily be used to enhance the grail quest, and it is readily obtainable. However, other methods of divination are equally important. Look in the further references for specific books on such techniques as the I Ching, Runes, Star+Gate, and *The Crystal Tree*.

The Tarot

Vivid, complex, delicately and intricately structured, the Tarot is one of the most popular psychic arts. Each of its 78 cards has a range of up to a dozen meanings, depending on whether the card is reversed or upright, what other cards are near it, and where it falls in a spread. If this sounds complicated, it is. However, it is also a rewarding study for anyone interested in learning the basic skills and disciplines of psychic work. Of the traditional psychic arts, only the mathematical beauties and shifting patterns of astrology come close to Tarot's depth and richness of meaning.

The Tarot, with its complex symbolic structure, incorporates the four elements, numerology, and astrology and is also intimately connected with the Kabbalah and the Tree of Life. There is, unfortunately, no room here to discuss all these links and connections; they are dealt with more fully in *The Crystal Tree* (available from Whitford Press, a division of Schiffer Publishing). The discussion here will be confined to the major arcana and how they can help you find the inner grail.

The Major Arcana

The 22 cards of the major arcana are the most powerful cards of the Tarot. They are a progression of symbols that lead the initiate from desire to fulfillment, ignorance to knowledge, and selfish isolation to union with the Universe. Each card expresses the spiritual truth of a certain step along the Path. There are no suits in the major arcana, as there are in the minor arcana. Each card stands on its own, but it is also part of a particular and meaningful order: from 0, the Fool (which begins the usual progression but properly fits before and after every card), to 21, the World (which ends the spiral in perfect balance)--and then the Fool begins it all again.

The twin themes--the poles--of the major arcana are balance and change. To find balance you must change; when balance is found, change rapidly alters it. Constantly changing direction and constantly moving upward, swung back in a circle on the central pole of balance/change, the only path possible is a spiral. The feminine manifestation of God is often called a spinner; we, like thread, are spinning ourselves upward on that spindle, the polar opposites united, balance/change. Like shellfish we expand our shells or die; many seashells grow in a spiral pattern, and they are a universal symbol of life and resurrection. Our spiral path is mapped by the major arcana.

Each of the cards represents a step on the path, an archetypal force that must be dealt with. Each will be discussed in order, beginning with the Fool, who starts out on the quest, and ending with the World, the transfigured self, in balance with the Universe, that in perfect freedom serves God.

A Note on Gender

The 22 cards of the major arcana include people, concepts, and inanimate objects. We can easily identify the concepts and the inanimate objects as archetypal forces working in our lives, but the people may present more of a puzzle. Gender is so important that many men feel uncomfortable identifying with the female cards, and many women feel uncomfortable identifying with the male cards. But each card--male or female, concept or object--symbolizes a force that is within every one of us.

In Jungian psychology no one is entirely male or female. Everyone has an inner self of the opposite sex: the animus (for women) or the anima (for men). A woman's animus or a man's anima is a deep source of the symbols found in the major arcana. In addition, women carry internal images of their fathers--the introjected father--as men carry introjected mothers. (For that matter, men carry introjected fathers and women introjected mothers.) Instead of being solidly one thing or the other, we are like the yin-yang symbol, which shows a circle of light in the dark side and a circle of darkness in the light side.

An example may be of help. Someone of either sex can identify with the Empress. Men and women can think of the Empress as the intro-jected mother. Women may express her mother qualities more directly in their own lives, but men also bear this nurturing, powerful woman within. Likewise, men may readily identify with the Emperor's paternal authority and discipline, but women also bear the Emperor in themselves and need to understand, accept, and express him.

An important part of our task in developing the self is learning to come to grips with this hidden self and to express it properly in daily life. The Tarot symbols briefly explicated here may give you some clues about how to accept and express these vital aspects of yourself.

THE FOOL

The Fool, numbered zero, signifies new beginnings, jumping into things, steps on a spiritual journey. He is pictured as heedless of any danger and ready to step gaily off a cliff. That fall may be a fortunate fall; it could lead him into places he never dreamed of going. The Fool's recklessness is not the stupid bravado of a drunk who insists on driving; it springs from innocent faith. Though he does not and cannot know what will happen to him, he ventures forth anyway; he is willing to let things happen.

It is easy to scorn the Fool and plume ourselves on our superior foresight, but consider for a moment. Do we know what will happen to us on every step of our lives? The answer--if we are honest--is no. The unexpected can always happen. The Fool at least acknowledges that truth, and his willingness to accept experience is an antidote to the stultifying sense of despair, failure, and claustrophobia of the life with-out a quest.

The Fool explores. He goes forth, seeking. He is the prototype of all of us who quest; he is Parsival, the quester of the Grail story. The Fool, in his wisdom, escapes the deadliness of the prepackaged, generic life--the life that substitutes conformity and convention for true self-expres-sion. Such lives are not so much lived as plotted out by a rigid and mindless timetable (marry by 25; make partner by 30; baby by 35; retire by 55) that never considers individual needs and differences.

All too often people who have accepted this kind of life awaken in their 40s to the realization that they have never lived as they wanted to but have swallowed the TV dinner life provided by their culture. A blue-collar worker may suddenly realize that she is starving for the college education denied her. A wealthy establishment lawyer may suddenly remember that he once wanted to do more than make money--he wanted to make music. Faced with such situations, people do one of three things: break out with an affair (assuming that a change of spouse will settle their uneasiness); do nothing and suffer the physical and emotional consequences of misery and unfulfillment (despairing of ever changing their lives); change their lives (knowing that there is not only no time like the present, but also there is no time *but* the present). Those who take the third way may be called fools, trying to turn their lives around at such a late stage. Indeed, they have heeded the call of the Fool, but whatever they suffer, however they change their lives, they fare better than their cynical or despairing brethren.

It takes the Fool's daring--as well as his ignorance--to move on; he never knows where he is going, and no more do we.

THE MAGICIAN

The Magician turns dreams into realities. Having accepted the Fool's willingness to fall, to fail, to try new things, you become the Magician by learning to identify what you truly want. (A great deal of your work in this book has been directed toward learning who you are and what you want.)

Yet mere selfishness is not enough. The self-actualization described here leads ultimately to a spiritual goal: becoming what God intended you to be. That is the point where the Magician can go astray. He can be the priestly mage, performing mighty miracles, or he can be a confidence trickster, cheating the crowd of their pennies. His destiny depends on the balance between self-realization and the Universe. In balance, the individual and the Universe dance together. Out of balance, the individual becomes a mere breathing, toiling zombie with no personality and no hope, a cipher who has abandoned self-realization; or a monster of selfishness, an insanely greedy ego demanding ever more power and gratification.

The central concern of the Magician is power. Power can be a dirty word. It has connotations of violence, brutality, manipulation. Power is the police state hauling away dissidents in cattle cars; power is the plutocrat bankrupting the small, independent competitor; power is the knife-wielding rapist forcing the victim to say she likes it. Many gentle people, seeing such horrors, have entirely abjured power. Yet we live by power. Turning dreams into reality demands it. So does the quest itself: the power to see, think, choose, resist. Electricity powers the computer I am writing this on, the music playing on the radio, the lamp that lights this room. Should I refuse to use electricity because it also delivers the death penalty in this state?

The distinction that must be made--not just here on the page, but in your life--is between *power over* and *power to*: between the quest for dominance and the quest for competence. *Power over* is the Shadow of *power to*. The power the Magician offers can be of either type. You must choose the kind of power you will use. Dominance offers certain satisfactions--not necessarily the overt sadism of the rapist, the plutocrat, the death-camp commandant--but the satisfaction of knowing that you are the best and others are not as good. Such satisfaction is precarious, however. It depends not only on your own strength but on others' weakness, and it must ultimately end as you age and lose your strength, your mental agility, your beauty, or whatever you have been priding yourself on. Competence may take you just as far in terms of achievement, but your satisfaction relies on joy in the thing itself rather than in your own preeminence in it. Not only does this sort of power offer more scope for joy--you can find satisfaction in others' achievements as well as in your own--but it also lasts forever. Dominance is destructive, envious, isolating; competence is constructive, generous, companionable.

The Magician can use either dominance or competence to turn dreams into reality. Your choice of one aspect of power over the other determines the path your quest will take.

THE HIGH PRIESTESS

The Magician is focused on power. The High Priestess is more concerned with being than with doing. She focuses not on external achievements but on the riches of the interior life. If the Magician gives you the power to turn dreams into reality, the High Priestess is the source of dreams.

The High Priestess is a woman of silence, learning, solitude; indeed, in the biblical book of Proverbs she is called Wisdom. Her role is like that of Diana, Isis, and all the other virgin goddesses. She is protector and slayer of the night creatures and wild animals, repository of memory and wisdom. The High Priestess lives in the unconscious, the psychic, and the creative parts of the mind, in the interior, silent places. Everyone needs a *temenos*--a sacred grove, a sheltered place where dark things can come into the light. The High Priestess, in the dark places of the mind, holds memory, weaves new images and ideas, studies the Torah (which is not only the first five books of Moses). From the darkness comes her wisdom.

The need for such retreats is beginning to be realized. Few people's lives allow space and time for reflection and dreaming. Most of us don't even get enough sleep. We can return refreshed and strengthened from a weekend away at a retreat or a spiritually oriented seminar. Even a solitary day spent walking the beach in winter can give you a taste of peace.

In our culture, more people are committed too much to the Magician's pursuit of power and not enough to the inner life of the High Priestess than the reverse. Yet it is possible to spend too much of your life inside your own head. If it is done properly, a mostly contemplative life can be extraordinarily fulfilling. The risk is the selfishness of solitude. Being uninvolved with other people can do more than encourage eccentricity. It can result in a kind of paralysis. Things are thought and not done; the imaginative life flourishes, while the faculties of action and force atrophy to the point that one cannot act even in an emergency. The recluse forgets how to speak, how to respond, how to love. The self becomes the only object in the Universe.

Though one goal of the quest is self-realization, the other is achieving balance with the Universe. The dance requires two partners. The High Priestess dances erratically when she dances alone. If she should dance with the Magician, their balance and power can give extraordinary fulfillment.

THE EMPRESS

The Fool is sexless and perhaps prepubescent. The Magician and the High Priestess are single, probably virgins. They belong to themselves and can give their whole attention to power or spirit. But the Empress and the Emperor are married. They deal not only with their own desires but also with the needs of other people. They are responsible.

The Empress is a woman in the fullness of strength. Her power is not limited to fertility, but fertility--the ability to create new life--does guide her actions. She is always conscious not only of the present but also of the future, not only of present actions but also of ideal standards. The Empress dedicates herself to creating, nurturing, shaping, and perfecting life.

The Empress embodies responsible love. She takes good care of her husband, her children, her home, her world. She is not merely a mother; she is Mother Nature, the Great Mother, the Goddess. She keeps house on a cosmic level: the balance of nature; the sea's self-cleansing; the whole terrifying cycle of natural birth, death, and renewal are under her hand. Any culture that lacks respect for the Empress will end up buried under slabs of concrete that worsen the floods (having filled in the wetlands and covered any other earth that could absorb the spring rains); breathing air dense enough to support a concrete freeway (which is, oddly enough, how the air got so thick in the first place); eating food with no resemblance whatsoever to what our Mother used to make (I doubt that she even recognizes some of the freeze-dried, chemically treated, and artifically colored products as the fruits of her Earth); and scorching to death under its own sun (having ripped away the veil of ozone provided to protect us).

Respect for the Empress leads to a life lived in harmony with others and with the Earth. She--the Empress in your own soul--endows you with decent values, guides you with loving discipline, nurtures you with care and independence, whichever you need at the time. A positive Empress is one of the best of inner resources. But--witness our dying planet--many people hate and fear the Empress. They do not see her strength and wisdom. They see the negative Empress.

A negative Empress image is the devouring mother: the one who created, who can also destroy. The devouring may be overt destruction-- physical violence, criminal neglect, even actual incest--or more subtle ways of weakening, controlling, or destroying her offspring. The mother who will not let her children grow up is a devouring mother; in order to retain her identity as a mother, she keeps her children babyish and dependent instead of encouraging them to mature. To do so, she may sap their strength through overindulgence and overmothering, making all choices and decisions for them so that they never learn to take care of themselves. She may control through guilt, becoming the mother-martyr, who bled and suffered to bear a child and will never let the kid forget it, or the mother who gave up a fine career, all her own ambitions, in order to raise a pack of ungrateful brats.

A devouring mother may brutalize her children with hateful words: They are worthless, stupid, useless, evil; with words like edged weapons she abuses those who depend upon her for life itself, and her dire prophecies of their doom usually come true. She hates her children's dependency, their weakness, their need of her, when she herself needs so much. Another may seduce her children (sometimes physically, more often symbolically) in order to prevent them from ever leaving her. Yet another devouring mother desires to make her children over in her own mold. Unable to fulfill her own ambitions, she forces her children to be what she could not be instead of what they themselves need to be.

All these negative images center around one or another manifestation of the same problem: The mother cannot let her children be separate people. It is understandable. A child grows inside a woman for nine months, breathes her breath and is fed by her blood. When it is born it suckles at her breast. As it grows it depends on her for everything. The baby is bone of her bone and flesh of her flesh; no one can be related more intimately. It came out of her. It is hers. The tearing away of such a scrap of the self and its transformation into a being that differs from and even opposes its maker and mother can be devastating, especially if the mother bases all her self-definition and all her self-esteem on her motherhood.

If the Empress is wife as well as mother, if she has other kinds of power and others ways to achieve self-realization, this can be among the most positive of archetypes. The Great Mother is powerful and responsible, balanced between her own inner needs and the needs of her children and her spouse. Involvement with other people--the kind of involvement that neither the Magician nor the High Priestess can manage--always carries some risks with it. The Empress, when properly lived out as part of the psyche, can be extraordinarily enhancing. Her respect for the Earth and the needs of others, her essential responsibility and good stewardship, her inclusive love and caring discipline, are all necessary for a happy adult life.

THE EMPEROR

The Emperor symbolizes the self-respect derived from ruling and controlling yourself. Because he is his own master, he is an emperor; worldly wealth and position have nothing to do with his spiritual power. Moreover, because he is in that position of strength he is able to have mercy over others; an emperor has the power to pardon criminals. He is just and generous; he is a strong and loving husband whose first concern is to keep his household together in harmony. "Husband" means houseband, the one who holds things together. As a verb "husband" still means to watch over, guard, keep careful account of. His role as spouse is far more than the paltry role of breadwinner. He is a loving, full partner in the raising of children and the concerns of business. These archetypes reflect the ancient tradition of both spouses working together on a farm or in a small business, not the modern tradition of the commuting husband and the wife stranded in suburbia or even the two-career marriage in which the spouses work not only away from each other but also away from home and children.

The Emperor is a father archetype as the Empress is a mother archetype. Their positive aspects are remarkably similar; good parenting from either father or mother consists of loving and accepting the child as a separate being; showing appropriate concern and care for the child's welfare and safety; and keeping an understandable, consistent, and attainable level of discipline. The differences between the negative images are interesting. The Empress errs in the direction of nonseparation from the child she bore in her womb; the Emperor errs in the opposite direction, assuming that his part is played and over when the sperm leaves his body. The devouring mother consumes her child in an effort to keep that initial closeness; the devouring father eats his offspring because he feels no more love and concern for it than he would for any other piece of meat. Indeed, the devouring father is often jealous of the child's closeness to the mother.

The devouring father--a figure neglected in modern psychology--embodies the Shadow of the Emperor's protective role. The strength meant to guard offspring is turned against them in physical or emotional violence. Such a man is impatient with the frailties and minor peccadilloes of childhood. He reacts with explosive rage to any indication of weakness or naughtiness, and his punishments would flatten a grown man, much less a shivering child. He resents and neglects his role in supporting his children. Instead of inspiring love in his children, he evokes a mixture of loathing and terror that can scar them for life. They go in fear of being killed by the man who should be their protector.

The negative father archetype is tragically common. Because children are now more or less raised in a fatherless world (except for those few children raised on farms), they have no image of male strength, no ideal of that strength used except in punitive action. Instead of the Emperor, we have Rambo; instead of the loving, protective husband and father we have men whose children are strangers even before the divorce. Psychological studies have shown that men who take care of their children in infancy are far less likely to abuse them or commit incest when the children are older. Early child care forges a bond stronger than rage or desire.

What happens to a culture that loses its respect for the Emperor? Its men become violent, irresponsible, unfeeling. They are unwilling to make a commitment. They hate women and regard children as a nuisance and not their responsibility. Child abuse and child molestation become common; after all, children are weak and available, and men without a strong Emperor archetype have no restraint on them to make them protect the weak. Instead, they exploit the weak.

The positive Emperor is self-disciplined; his strength--and he is very strong--is used for positive things. Without that self-discipline masculine strength can be unbelievably destructive. But self-discipline alone does not explain the Emperor. He is dedicated--as is the Empress--to a cause beyond himself, to the maintaining of a home and the rearing of children. The only explanation of that dedication is love. The Emperor loves and guides his children, and thus he does not rape or batter them. He loves and needs his wife, and he treats her with the same respect and concern that she offers him. We need more of him and less of Rambo, more who embody the knight's ideal of courage and gentleness.

THE HIEROPHANT

The Hierophant is an instructor in spiritual matters. He initiates the neophyte into the mysteries of the spiritual life, teaches the necessary rituals and chants, and acts as confessor and guide. He symbolizes the structure of faith and belief. The card has an undeserved reputation for self-righteous stuffiness, perhaps because the word *hierophant* is not in common use, perhaps because it is a specifically religious image and some influential occultists distrust organized religion. (If the card were called the Guru, its role would probably be more easily understood and accepted.) The Hierophant also represents your own standards of conduct. When you compare what you know you should do with what you are actually doing, you can be galvanized into change.

Without the Hierophant, without internal standards of right and wrong, the self is lost. Shifting standards and the desire to be liked and accepted--also known as peer pressure--dictate behavior. The whole grail search is based on discovering who you are, what you believe, and what you want to do with your life, regardless of convention. The Hierophant gives you the inner strength and the spiritual treasures that enable you to be your best self.

A too-rigid Hierophant can make you joyless; a too-lax Hierophant can make you wishy-washy. Clearly, the Hierophant must be kept strong and balanced in order to act as the bulwark of moral, ethical, and spiritual truths.

THE LOVERS

The Lovers is undoubtedly a card of love--falling in love, learning what is important both in love and in a lover--but is more a card of making proper choices in all areas of life. The original design of the Lovers (still used in such decks as the Marseilles Tarot) shows a young man choosing between an older woman and a younger one. This picture has Freudian overtones of choosing between the mother and the lover; in general, it deals with separation from parents as well as the other issues and choices of growing up.

Choice is a concept allied with the moral structure the Hierophant provides. The Hierophant gives the standards by which the choice will be made; the Lovers give the opportunity to choose. This card represents the crossroads in the self--the conflicting desires to have both childish indulgence and adult privileges, to have both security and independence, to be loved without giving commitment and to be married without suffering restrictions. You cannot eat your cake and have it too; you must choose. The choice is embodied here in the Lovers. The choice of a spouse is, of course, a central concern, but the choice of adulthood over childishness extends far beyond the plain issue of marriage.

Essentially, you will make your choices by those standards and desires that are most dear to you. You can thus examine your choices to discover what has really been first in your life. If there is a consistent split between what you say you want and what you actually choose, you may not be as committed to those standards or desires as you think. If there is a split between theory and practice, it is probably to be found here, at the Lovers. Go back and look at the Hierophant, the Emperor and Empress, the Magician and the High Priestess. Where have you lost your balance? You can mend such splits in the self; indeed, you must. The integrity you strive for is nothing more or less than wholeness.

THE CHARIOT

This card is an image of control: the charioteer holds the reins of two sphinxes. The discipline of the Chariot is the self-control pictured here, for the sphinxes are the charioteer's own body and soul, conscious and unconscious minds, good intentions and selfish temptations. In order to do creative work, you must be in control of yourself; in order to have a happy marriage (or other strong commitment), the partners must each put the commitment above individual needs and desires in order to work together.

Control is rather a static image, but the Chariot is far from static. It moves, and it moves fast. But it cannot move at all unless both horses are harnessed and pulling together, unless the charioteer holds every rein true. This image perfectly symbolizes the need to get your life together, to keep different forces not just in balance but pulling together in a common purpose. You must organize all the parts of your life by the same principles or parts of you will be pulling in different directions.

Why is that so bad? A classic example from nature expresses it best. A small lizard called the skink is sometimes born with two heads, but since the two heads can never agree to go in the same direction after food or away from danger, the double-headed skink usually dies very early. The Chariot can come up against the same problem. Unless you are whole, you will be constantly pulling against yourself, defeating your own purpose. Like a car stuck in the mud, you will spin your wheels instead of getting somewhere. Without the wholeness the Chariot represents, you will not be able to muster the strength to achieve. From fragmentation comes frustration and despair.

The image of the Chariot is the image of integrity: having a whole unbroken self. If you believe in honesty, all your life must be honest; you cannot expect to cheat on your spouse or swipe office supplies and still be honest. If you believe in love toward your neighbor, you cannot love everybody except a selected few. Although you may not feel sentimental attachment to everyone, you must give everyone the same respect, courtesy, and consideration.

None of this is easy. Driving a chariot is skilled work; getting your life in order is very difficult indeed--even with the aid of God--and nearly impossible on your own. But the ideal exists so we can strive for it. The Chariot shows how smoothly and with what power we were meant to move.

JUSTICE

Justice, like the Chariot, is a card of balance, but the balance here seems static compared to the control and energy of the Chariot. Yet the Chariot deals with controlling yourself by living a life of principles. The card Justice deals with exercising your principles in a wider arena. Justice is a social card, and it shows the need for balance and fairness in dealings with other people.

Justice--a basic sense of fair play, of other people's rights--enables us to live in society. It regulates such apparently minor courtesies as standing patiently in line, giving up a seat to an older person or a pregnant woman, holding doors for those who come after you or for people laden with packages or small children. Among the magnificent persons and the profound concepts we have seen so far, Justice seems like pretty small potatoes. But let's examine the world without Justice.

The society without a sense of Justice usually clamors loudly for absolute fairness in everything, but fairness in these cases is defined as privilege for the self and screw the others. New York City is the stereotyped example of a city without Justice; though many individuals there have a strong sense of fair play, the city itself lives up to all the awful stories. Every encounter is a struggle for dominance and advantage. Everything you do is a direct assault on someone else. Life there is a zero-sum game, where everything you win is taken away from someone who loses. The best you can hope for is a draw. Even then both combatants walk away with a sense of grievance that they will take out on the next person they see. And so forth, until the ill will and resentment could fill the world. It is, in fact, very much like the description of hell in C. S. Lewis's *The Screwtape Letters* and *The Great Divorce*.

How--outside of hell--does a society get that way? What feeds Justice in individuals? Justice springs from magnanimity (literally "great soul"). If you have enough in yourself, you can share with others. If you are whole, you can afford to give. Without all the qualities of discipline, high principles, loving responsibility, proper use of power, balance between doing and being (discussed in the previous cards of the major arcana), no one can have Justice. New York is so appalling for probably two reasons: (1) the physical conditions of the city, the overcrowding and buildings of inhuman scale that deprive people of a sense of their own worth and make it obvious that the sunlight stolen from you is going to your undeserving neighbor; and (2) the dreadful disparity between the wealthiest and the poorest classes. This makes it seem impossible to change your own station in life by hard work. Nothing you do can have any effect in such a vast and inhuman place. Even if you could get out and get a decent education, you could never be one of *them*. Other factors include the obvious contempt of the rich for the poor and the excessively high value placed on wealth.

Individual wholeness can make for individual Justice. Societal integrity is the source of social Justice. A society with integrity does not indulge in prejudice and discrimination. Instead of worshiping status and conspicuous consumption, it respects honest labor. It offers equal opportunity to all: an excellent education to all the children; a chance to work hard and advance to everyone, whatever their race, color, creed, gender, age, or social status.

THE HERMIT

With Justice the soul learns to live in society. The Hermit goes back toward solitude, not from selfishness or hatred of others, but out of love for God. The Hermit knows that personal wholeness can sometimes best be fostered by solitude, and he (or she) goes inward toward the mountains and deserts of the self, where he/she can learn and grow without distraction. The Hermit is truly androgynous; though the card usually shows an old man with a beard, many hermits were women who lived in solitude so they could contemplate God. Though few modern nuns are hermits, the cloistered orders offer a contemplative life of silence and solitude.

Some people (usually women, who are taught to be responsible for others' welfare) feel a deep conflict between their inner Hermit, which yearns for solitude, and the social demands of Justice. How can they be reconciled?

The answer lies in proportion. Very few people need or want to be the Hermit all their lives or even for very long stretches at a time. Most of us express the Hermit in an occasional free evening or solitary weekend. The need to be alone is balanced with the need to see and be involved with others. Both are important. It is possible to take a break now and then. Social responsibility does not demand 24-hour-a-day devotion to others; even motherhood needs a rest (maybe especially motherhood).

If you learn to accept the Hermit in yourself, you will plan for enough time alone to keep yourself sane and serene. Remember, the call of the Hermit is a call to the holy in yourself. Answering that call is as much a duty as helping others. Moreover, in a practical sense constant devotion to others becomes an impossibility without time for the spirit. You do the world and yourself no favor when you drive yourself to the point of collapse. Martyrdom may be gratifying to some, but the ones for whom the martyr is sacrificed usually resent being cast in the role of persecutor.

What if the Hermit calls you to longer spells of solitude, to a turning toward God and solitude? Look again at the card. The Hermit, carrying a lantern, is walking alone on the heights. If there are people below, he does not know it; he is concentrating on God and the path at his feet. Yet anyone below would see his light and know that there was a higher path. If the Hermit had stayed down among the crowds of the marketplace, his lantern would not have illuminated anything--it might have even set fire to something in the crush. The Hermit, though withdrawn from the world, may lead better than someone in the thick of the fray. Remember Thomas Merton, a Trappist monk whose thoughts on peace reached the world. Sometimes the life most dedicated to solitude is richest in meaning and virtue.

THE WHEEL OF FORTUNE

Long before the Wheel of Fortune was a word game on television, it was a symbol of the changing fortunes of life. The Wheel of Fortune symbol-izes the haphazardness of the worldly world, and the meaninglessness and mutability of social status and other merely external conditions of life. Its form--the perpetually spinning circle--suggests the Earth itself in shape and movement. Its meaning is also clear: It represents the changes that come to all of us in turn, the uncertainties and the varying luck that can drastically alter the lot of even the most stable, staid, steady person. But there is a deeper underlying meaning: The growth of the individual relies on change.

Too often we think of ourselves and our fates as something steady and unchangeable. When changes come we resent them, or we panic, and we must be dragged kicking and screaming into the new life. Grief, fear, and anger over forced changes are natural reactions; nevertheless, you must move beyond them to an acceptance of the change and a willingness to see the good in the new situation. The Wheel of Fortune, like all the other cards of the major arcana, is not just an external influ-ence. The Wheel of Fortune is within you as well, telling you when the time comes for you to move on, to make changes, to turn from one archetype to another. No healthy life stays always at the Fool or the Lovers or the Hermit. Your life will probably tend to emphasize one over another, but all must have some influence. Refusing to move on from the warm embrace of the Empress into more dangerous or adven-turous ground is as ultimately destructive as refusing to be weaned would be.

The Wheel of Fortune asks you to change, to move on. If you come back--and you probably will--it will be at a higher level. How can you refuse?

STRENGTH

Having learned about the need for change and the cyclical nature of reality, you may then find Strength. The card Strength shows a woman holding the mouth of a lion. The meaning is implicit in her serene confidence and power while she handles the noble, dangerous creature. The card is the symbol for internal balance between the physical and spiritual, but it also indicates a balance between the world and the indi-vidual soul.

Strength is the poised, balanced self that already knows the proper priorities. This self is strong enough to make manipulation and emotional blackmail impossible. The person with Strength will neither submit to them nor impose them on others. Strength turns the Magician's Faustian quest for power inside out. Instead of seeking power so it can be like God, it seeks godliness--knowing and serving the proper spiritual priorities--and as a result attains power. This power is not wasted on competition and dominance, but is generously shared with everyone in need.

Strength prevents self-pity, though not grief or pain. Strength conquers but may not banish fear. Strength does not make the world wonderful and life easy; it gives vision to see the joy of the world as well as the pain, and it gives courage to deal with pain. Strength offers endurance, magnanimity, the willingness to go on.

What is life without Strength? Despair. When horrors overwhelm you, when fate seems malignant, when nothing will ever get better, Strength carries you through. It enables you to bear pain as well as feel joy. Without it, life is bleak indeed.

THE HANGED MAN

The Hanged Man is a difficult card in any context. It goes against all the grain of ordinary thought. It makes no sense. The Hanged Man seems to be a holy fool, or maybe just a fool, hanging from a tree by his foot. But remember what we have already learned about the rapid changes possible under the Wheel of Fortune, about the endurance and courage embodied in Strength. The Hanged Man calls on both. He endures; he waits out the changes, but he suffers all the way through them. The pain is real, but it ends. The rewards of the pain are real, and they last.

The Hanged Man is the dying god who suffers for the sake of wisdom. In the most ultimate sense, in the highest form, it is the card of Christ. Others, mythical and real, follow in His footsteps and suffer likewise. The Hanged Man is Odin, who hung nine nights on the world tree Yggdrasil in order to win the runes--magic words, the alphabet, poetry--for his people. This is the card of all who sacrifice themselves, all who do what is right, even though they know they will suffer, and then endure the suffering. Though the suffering may not always extend to death, it does sometimes. Joan of Arc saved France, though she burned for it. Gandhi used nonviolent means to free India; he was assassinated.

Also assassinated were Abraham Lincoln, Martin Luther King, Jr., and the Kennedy brothers. Simone Weil, philosopher and mystic, died of her beliefs. Even those who do not pay the ultimate price for their beliefs pay some price in tears, suffering, loneliness, scorn.

People naturally recoil from this kind of sacrifice. It is morbid, excessive, unnecessary, dramatic. Yet such pain and sacrifice are not only necessary, but they also are commonplace. It is not the outcome--actual, physical death--that makes this card so powerful; it is the willingness to give everything to a cause greater than the self. Its ordinary forms may surprise you: a dancer practicing until her muscles ache; a parent saying no to a child's unreasonable demands; a dieter pushing away a slice of cheesecake. All are making sacrifices to a higher cause. The dancer seeks perfection in grace and motion; the parent wants to raise a responsible child, not a spoiled brat; the dieter wants a slimmer form.

The Hanged Man is usually interpreted as being of good luck to people who do creative work. The link is that willingness to sacrifice for an unseen goal. A writer makes a commitment to create something out of nothing--to produce 300 pages of finished, polished prose out of some ink; some paper; and years of thought, effort, research, writing, and revising. A sculptor takes a featureless block of clay or stone and finds the statue within. Any artist suffers and works for years to reach the level of skill that will capture even a shadow of the original conception. Artists sacrifice themselves and all the other things they could do with their time in order to create art.

Most people are not artists, are not willing or able to sacrifice everything else to achieve greatness. But everyone makes small sacrifices. Everyone learns ultimately that the Hanged Man's foolishness, his taking of the hard road, is the only path in the end to fulfillment.

DEATH

Death is another difficult card. In divination Death is not physical death --you cannot foretell physical death with the Tarot. The card Death is both death and resurrection. It is the necessary, often painful end of one stage of life and the beginning of another. Yes, Death is the result of the kind of sacrifice made by the Hanged Man. Leaving home is a death-and-resurrection experience, and so are marrying, retiring from a job, and many other physical and spiritual experiences. Sometimes you know such an experience is coming; at other times, it overtakes you like lightning and you walk away reborn.

Some of the inescapable terror of Death lies in the resurrection. You cannot know what and who you will be when the experience is over and you are reborn. But you are always resurrected as yourself: yourself wiser, less naive, more considerate, somehow different. The parable of the grain of wheat illustrates this. The grain must fall into the ground and die, and when it is resurrected, it is different. It is no longer a seed but a plant bearing many seeds. The thought of the differences may frighten you, but you can endure.

As we saw when we considered the element air, communication requires separation. Sometimes Death is that necessary separation. There must be some space; the changes Death brings--changes on many levels, changes that can be agonizing--open up new space. The new life is joyful, though the passage to it may be terrifying.

What happens if you refuse this death, if you would rather not change at all? Stagnation, bitterness, and increased fear result. Change becomes harder and harder the more you resist it. A life without renewal rapidly becomes a life without meaning or vigor--a kind of death-in-life far worse than Death and resurrection.

TEMPERANCE

Temperance is pictured as an angel, mixing waters in two chalices. Having endured Death and its consequent resurrection, you will see the need for balance with new eyes. You have changed, and the way you think and feel and act will change as well. Temperance enables you to make such changes lovingly. It gives a knowledge of priorities; you can now create a living, breathing balance between your needs and those of others, between the forces working in your soul and the real world you must live in.

Emotional stability and strength come not from rigidity but from rhythm, from the ability to dance with the Universe. Temperance teaches you to do that. It enhances strength and self-esteem, because these qualities come from the ability to see yourself and others in the proper light. When you understand that lives shift and change, but that there is a pattern to all the changes, you have reached the flowing peace and kinetic balance of Temperance.

THE DEVIL

The Devil in the Tarot is not Lucifer, also known as Satan. It is a symbol of all the faults, temptations, fears, and guilt that keep us in bondage, whether they exist in you or in other people.

In its role as the (so to speak) interior Devil--your unexpressed fears and nightmares, the violence you have suffered, the hidden knowledge of the harm you have done to others--it is compounded of both the wrongs you have done to others and the wrongs that have been done to you. Together these work to destroy your self-esteem, because they are hidden (your deepest secrets) and because you are ashamed of having hurt others and of having been hurt yourself. Ultimately you may come to identify all these hidden horrors as your true self, and you begin to feel as loathsome as your inner secret.

It is called the Devil because it chains you with your consent. All of that can be forgiven and has no real power except what you consent to give it, just as Satan has no power over someone who has asked for God's protection. Yet there are times when the inner demon drives you to seek out goodness, to forgive and to ask for forgiveness, to get help to erase the horrors. How? By making you so miserable that the only alternative is to change, to understand and examine the secret, to forgive yourself and others. In that way the suffering can be turned to good use; later you will be able to help others by drawing on your own painful experiences.

The "exterior" Devil--the faults and sins of the world--can stimulate change by showing you the results of your own faults in someone else. If you have a minor drug habit, seeing someone in the last throes of heroin or cocaine addiction can shock you into giving it up. If you cannot control your temper, a clear sight of the destructiveness of violence--a murder trial, even the sight of someone bruised and bleeding from an enraged attack--can teach you that there are better ways to handle anger.

All this may seem harsh and painful. Who wants to deal with faults or recognize them as being destructive to him/herself and others? But look again at that last paragraph. There are worse things than making the painful effort to change.

THE TOWER

The Tower is a frightening image of lightning striking a high tower. Two people are falling from the riven tower. Yet this card can be a symbol of new hope, for the Tower destroys only in order to build. It clears the way for new and more appropriate edifices. The revelations of the Devil have probably shown you what you need to change in yourself; the Tower will carry out that change. If, for example, the Devil has shown you to be in bondage to your childhood suffering, the Tower will help you clear out that pain and build anew. You need not--you must not!-- throw your parents off a tower, but you have to throw your suffering off. You have to feel it, see it, and end it.

Without the Tower, you remain locked in the dungeon with the Devil. You need to walk away from sin and pain, go out into that high clean place, and become free. This process is not easy--has anything worth doing been easy? But the freedom and self-knowledge it gives is irreplaceable.

THE STAR

The Star is one of the loveliest cards of the major arcana, both in design and meaning. It signifies strong attachments between people who are not related by blood; just as the constellations, whose power is so manifest in the science of astrology, are connected only by our perceptions of them. In the same way the friendships and passions of the Star are connected only by perceived affinity, perceived goodness. There is no blood tie. That kind of love relies on communication, a balance of privacy and sharing, and freedom to express the self.

Love is a kind of gravity: too close, and the swinging orbs crash and die; too far, and they miss one another entirely. At the proper distance they create a binary star of intense magnitude. The Star expresses that exact distance, the equation of love.

THE MOON

The Moon offers both mystery and madness, passion and poetry. It is a virgin huntress who calls you to unleash your instincts and a mother who reminds you of things you would rather forget. The Moon gives you psychic visions. The Moon gives you dreams.

The link between all these dreams and mysteries, instincts and memories, is the unconscious mind, which keeps all these things until we are ready to deal with them. It is most often associated with the unpleasant things we have repressed: all the hidden, unforgiven sins and guilt. They surface again in one way or another: nightmares, neuroses, certain illnesses, for example. This process is not always what brings on illness and suffering, but the Moon--part of ourselves, not an outside force--automatically reacts to hidden shames and sins by trying to remind us of them so they can be confessed and forgiven. Because the unconscious cannot write us a letter, it can only work as clearly as it can through conscience (which is often ignored) and then through dreams. But how many people really listen to their own dreams? Through all the ways at its disposal, the unconscious tries to remind us that something is wrong, and we try to ignore that uncomfortable situation.

The Moon does more than punish, though. It also rewards with creativity, with joy, with clearer and clearer dreams as we listen more closely and try to understand, with inspiration, with balance and health. These are not rewards that other people can count--or steal--but they are infinitely satisfying.

THE SUN

The Sun is both the source and (in a lesser sense) the result of spiritual strength. It is a metaphor for divine love and power radiating outward from heaven; the holy rays feed us as actual sunlight feeds plants and trees. After learning to deal with the archetypal selves, with Death and resurrection, with the Devil and the Moon, the soul is ready to act as the Sun does--to feed and help others by the light it sheds.

The Sun is often referred to as a card of sacred marriage. A true marriage is based on the Sun's sharing of glory. Though partners must also share one another's burdens and help each other through difficulties and pain, the spiritual and physical consummation of marriage is the Sun's blazing, holy, and magnificent work. The Sun burns by fusion; so the power of marriage is in the making of one flesh from two, the linking of two souls in an eternal splendor.

Like the Sun, a true marriage blesses those around it with light, warmth, and life. A true marriage is not two people so involved with each other that they neglect the rest of the world. It is two people whose commitment to one another gives them strength and resources that they can share with the world. A true marriage is a haven for the spouses but also a center of hospitality for their friends and family and the stranger within the gates.

I am not suggesting that this is what marriage feels like; still less that a marriage should end if it does not feel like the Sun. Marriage is a commitment, and it is not always easy, pleasant, or fun. You cannot bail out because your partner is in a kind of pain that you cannot soothe. You cannot quit just because ordinary life--the cooking, the cleaning, the job, the children--leaves you feeling unromantic. In a sacred marriage--the true marriage intended to last forever--you have a duty and a responsibility to your partner, as well as rights and privileges. Again, like the Sun, a marriage does not go out because there are fogs or clouds or even night.

Given that indissoluble commitment, given that sense of divine blessing on your union, you will find that the minor irritations can work themselves out. The Sun promises new life. You can fulfill that promise.

JUDGMENT

Judgment symbolizes the end of the world, the results and rewards of the way each person has chosen to live, work, think, act, love, and be. Acts have meaning, and they therefore have results. Life is not a game but a spiritual journey. Judgment tells you where you have gone. It was perhaps best expressed in Galatians 6:7--"Whatsoever a man soweth, that shall he also reap."

In the short-term sense in which the card is usually found, it signifies a summing-up, a time for reflection and taking stock. It is a needed pause in the cycle to let you see how far you have come and where you think you might go next.

Those who live life without reflection tend to repeat the same mistakes over and over again, unconsciously trying to get it to come right this time. Judgment shows this. The reaping is done over and over again, always with the same crop of sorrow, disturbance, pain. Let Judgment help you take stock. Be honest with yourself. The only freedom, after all, comes from the truth.

THE WORLD

The World shows a woman with covered loins dancing in a circling wreath and surrounded by the four creatures that symbolize the gospels (and of course the four elements). The loin covering, however, hides the fact that she is a hermaphrodite: the ultimate symbol of balance. She/he may even be Tiresias, the Greek prophet, who became a woman when he found two snakes coupling--a symbol of the reuniting of all dualities. (Snakes are also considered a symbol of wisdom and renewal when associated with the Tree of Life; they symbolize evil only when associated with the Tree of Knowledge.) After seven years as a woman, Tiresias came upon the same snakes coupling again and was returned to manhood.

The World depicts the reconciliation of opposites (the major theme of the Tarot itself, with its emphasis on balance) and the wisdom gained by that reconciliation. We may reach it, but we cannot hope to keep it; we visit, glimpse, enjoy, and then go on to a new spiral, a new round of dealing with ourselves and the world. As a client of mine said, "I'm still fighting the same battles I fought ten and 20 years ago. But at least I'm fighting them on a higher plane."

The World sums up the dancing Universe and the balance of opposing forces that is not a dead stasis but a living, fluid equilibrium. It is the ultimate achievement, reaching that level of dancing peace where every step and every breath have a sacred meaning, where every pain and trouble reveals its purpose in the pattern of your life, where existence is kindled to glory, where "all that is not silence is music." This is a glimpse of the kingdom of heaven within. This, at long, long last, is the Grail.

USING THE TAROT FOR SELF-DISCOVERY

Having read all the symbolic meanings, you may be asking how these cards can specifically help you. They can help you if you meditate on their meanings. They can help if you heed their lessons. But the most specific way the Tarot can help is through divination. As indicated earlier, this book has neither the intention nor the space to fully explore divination for others; many other works have adequately handled that task. Our task here is the grail. How can you use divination to help you find the grail?

Get a Tarot deck (see the recommendations in Chapter 2) and separate out the major arcana. (If the deck is brand-new, it will be all in order.) Then shuffle the major arcana and cut it into three piles. While you shuffle, concentrate on the question or issue that is troubling you. Turn each pile over. The bottom card is the card you will read; read from right to left.

You will now have three cards facing you. Some may be upside down; this indicates a reluctance or block in dealing with that energy. Before you go back and read the sections on each card, look at them. Try to understand the symbols with the knowledge you have gleaned from this book and any other reading you have done. How do the cards make you feel? Can you see a link between them? Write down the three cards in the spaces provided; use an "R" afterwards to indicate reversed (up-side-down).

Date _____   Question _____

Card 1 _____

Card 2 _____

Card 3 _____

Then turn back to the interpretations and begin to see the links between the cards. Weave the influences into a story. Try to come up with different ways the forces could be connected. When you are satisfied with the interpretation, write it down in the space provided.

Interpretation _____

_____

_____

_____

_____

Tarot Records

Date _____   Question _____

Card 1 _____

Card 2 _____

Card 3 _____

Interpretation _____

_____

_____

_____

_____

Date _____   Question _____

Card 1 _____

Card 2 _____

Card 3 _____

Interpretation _____

_____

_____

_____

_____

Date _____   Question _____

Card 1 _____

Card 2 _____

Card 3 _____

Interpretation _____

_____

_____

_____

_____

Date _____   Question _____

Card 1 _____

Card 2 _____

Card 3 _____

Interpretation _____

_____

_____

_____

_____

Date _____   Question _____

Card 1 _____

Card 2 _____

Card 3 _____

Interpretation _____

_____

_____

_____

_____

Date _____   Question _____

Card 1 _____

Card 2 _____

Card 3 _____

Interpretation _____

_____

_____

_____

_____

SEEKING OTHERS' COUNSEL:
HOW TO CHOOSE A PSYCHIC

Sometimes readings for yourself are not enough to clarify what is going on in your life. You may have a question that you cannot be impartial about, or a complex problem that needs a lengthier, more detailed reading than you can give yourself. Sometimes you just need to talk to someone who will be compassionate, knowledgeable, and nonjudgmental. Then you need a psychic or reader (I use the words interchangeably here).

The best way to find a psychic is through the personal recommendation of a trustworthy friend, but there are other ways. Psychic fairs offer a choice of many readers using different techniques; I have had mostly good experiences with them. Renaissance fairs and even craft shows often feature psychics. The quality ranges from superb to fraudulent. Learn to use your own psychic abilities to see if you are attuned to the individual reader. You might also check with local metaphysical bookstores or even an astrology group; they should be able to recommend someone. Ads in local newspapers or metaphysical magazines can tell you a great deal. Many highly reputable psychics advertise, but you should check the ad carefully. Someone who promises you love, money, revenge, or freedom from curses is probably a fraud.

Note: The following discussion uses Tarot readers as an example. The principles apply to any reader or psychic, whether doing psychometry, palmistry, crystal gazing, tea leaf reading, or whatever. No one group is any more likely to be fraudulent than another.

Bad Psychics: Frauds and Incompetents

Frauds

Unfortunately, many readers are, quite frankly, skillful frauds. They may detect your weaknesses and play on them. Walk straight out the door if a reader tells you that you are under a curse that only he or she can remove. This revelation is a ploy, designed to fleece you of all the cash you have. You may be told you have a curse on your money and that it must be brought in to be cleansed--either by burning it or by putting it through a purifying ceremony. Trust me; your money will be neither burned nor ritually laundered. It will be stolen.

Perhaps the reader tells you that you might be under a curse. To make sure, he or she will send you home with a clear glass jar, to be filled with water and kept under your bed for a specific length of time. When you bring back the capped jar, the reader will usually sniff the contents or spit into the jar, then tighten the lid, wrap it in paper, and shake it vigorously. The clear water thereupon undergoes a horrifying transformation. It turns a nasty color (usually red) and weird things appear: snakes, hair, teeth, bones, whatever. The reader then informs you that you are definitely under a curse, and it will cost you a lot of money to remove that curse. But the color is vegetable dye; the disgusting contents may include plastic snakes, instant dried onion, perhaps some human hair and teeth. How did they get there? The reader dexterously switched jar lids while spitting into the jar. The revolting effects were glued with water-soluble glue to the underside of the new lid. The vigorous shaking freed them, and voilà: a curse.

I reveal these things so that if you inadvertently go to a fraud, you can recognize and avoid the traps laid for you. No one should be forced to undergo the kind of suffering a fraudulent psychic can cause. Frauds are utterly contemptible. They heartlessly terrorize the innocent and extort money; they may share private information about your life with other frauds so you are convinced of their powers. They abuse the client's trust and may drive a victim to despair or even suicide. They have given all psychics a bad name.

The typical victim is already vulnerable--lonely, nervous, unhappy, ill, distressed. One of my clients, recommended to me by a mutual friend, had been under the spell of such a fraud. Annie came to me on a bright October day quivering in terror--literally shaking. A reader had told her she would die at Christmas. Annie had already emptied her small savings account in an attempt to buy a reprieve from the death sentence, but the reader was inexorable. She needed more money to remove the curse. Annie had no more money, and she prepared to die by being cool and distant with her children, so they wouldn't miss her when she was gone. I explained how the fraudulent reader had played tricks on Annie and did a real reading for her. Still, even with reassurance, prayer, and emotional support, she remained terrified until Christmas was over.

The odd thing was that the reader had read cards for several other of my clients without telling them anything of the sort. She had recognized in Annie an ideal victim.

What are the signs of the fraud? He or she may do one or more of the following things:

--Tell you that you, your money, or your family are cursed.

--Advise or demand that you return very frequently.

--Charge inordinate rates for burning candles or "blessing" your possessions.

--Tell you that you or a family member will die on a specific date, especially if he or she offers to prevent or postpone the death.

--Tell you that you must keep secret everything that goes on during sessions.

--Threaten you with curses or other disasters if you discuss the sessions with anyone, if you miss a session, or if you visit another reader.

Let me take up these points one by one. I have already dealt with curses, but what about the second item? How often is too often?

That varies depending on circumstances. Many of my clients see me around their birthdays (a good time for readings), then perhaps once a season. Others come every four to six weeks. People make emergency appointments during times of crisis, of course. But anyone who tells you that you must come in daily or weekly is probably milking you. The two exceptions are when you going to a reader for teaching or counseling. Both these activities require regular and frequent sessions. If you are in apprenticeship--learning to deal with your own psychic powers; learning how to read cards, palms, runes, crystals, or whatever--you will probably see your teacher at least once a week. If you are seeing an astrologer or reader who is doing therapy with you, you will see them at stated intervals, exactly as you would any other therapist. But beware the ordinary reader who tells you that you need daily contact. Most reputable psychics are wary of clients who call every day or every week; the clients usually want the wrong things out of a reading, as discussed previously.

Charging inordinate rates is another variable. A highly skilled reader usually charges about as much as any other professional. At the time of writing, $30 to $50 for a half-hour reading, or $60 to $100 for an hour, is not unreasonable. You will pay more if you have a very illustrious reader. Some readers charge variable rates, depending on the client's circumstances. You are actually more likely to get in trouble with someone who charges only two dollars at the door but attempts extortion. Any fee for candle-burning or blessing of possessions is usually in order to get rid of curses--and again, a fraud.

What about death? There is a Death card, of course, and its interpretation was discussed earlier. But let me repeat this: *You cannot foretell physical death using Tarot cards*. The day of your death is not predetermined. Furthermore, the cards focus on spiritual changes rather than physical ones, and death *cannot* be determined. No reputable psychic-- even if an approaching death is sensed in another way--will ever tell you of it. Why? Because the chance of being mistaken is too great and no psychic is right 100 percent of the time. The potential psychological or physical damage is too great, and it simply isn't that cut and dried. People go through many times of increased risk before they actually die. Those times of illness or danger do show up; a good psychic may warn you that driving or flying may be especially hazardous, that there is a potential for illness, or that other risks are present. But the nature of foretelling is a foretelling of choices and possibilities. Death is just too definite an answer. It cannot be seen with certainty. Incidentally, foretelling a death is also illegal in some states.

The need for secrecy is another tip-off that you are being set up for fraud. This technique ensures that you are cut off from friends who may talk you out of spending thousands on removing curses. Though some psychics are uncomfortable with tape recorders, many will gladly let you tape the session or will even provide a tape as part of their service. You usually have the choice of being alone for your reading or bringing a friend. A reputable psychic, though, will not let strangers listen in on your session.

Threats of disaster are a further way of keeping unwary victims from sensible help while making sure they come back for more and more sessions. Secrecy is enforced by these threats, sometimes even after the victim has lost thousands to fraud. Further, a kind of shameful intensity is maintained between psychic and victim. The victim, unable to reality-test what is happening, is drawn further and further into the reader's lying version of reality and becomes increasingly more dependent on the psychic. Contact with friends and family is cut off, and the victim has no one to turn to but the victimizer. Contact with other psychics might break the spell by casting doubt on the fraud's pronouncements. Soon the victim is completely enmeshed and disoriented--ready to do whatever the fraud desires.

I might add here that not all frauds are done for money. Some are simply power games, played by a deranged or unscrupulous reader who enjoys manipulating others.

If you find yourself getting enmeshed, *get out*. If someone offers to purify your money, call the bunco squad. If someone says you are under a curse, go to the cops and then call a therapist, a clergyperson, a sensible friend. The number of people either desiring to or capable of casting a curse is infinitesimal. Further, and more important, *no curse can touch you without your permission*. Just say no.

Incompetents

What about the psychic who doesn't try to steal your cash or isolate you from your friends, but just doesn't do a good job?

Some are sincere but untrained. Some are cynically milking the latest fads and have no real knowledge. Some have erratic gifts. Some may simply be having a bad day.

The best defense against these people is knowledge. If you have trained your own psychic gifts, you may be able to detect the incompetent. (Be careful that you are really detecting it, not indulging your prejudices about looks, age, race, or whatever.) Don't forget the more conventional methods of choosing a reader: asking about the reader's ideas about psychic work, how long he or she has been practicing, who (if anyone) trained him or her. A college degree may not be any guarantee of skill, but years of psychic work may. If the reader seems ignorant of the basics or unwilling to answer questions, move on to another. Why waste your money?

Once you have chosen a reader, the more you know about the

method, the better off you will be. Individual readers develop their own shades of meaning for various cards, and some (perhaps most) information comes from the psychic flow rather than the cards. Nevertheless, a knowledgeable client can tell if the readings are manifestly perverse with regard to what the cards say. You can even give yourself a good reading if you are stuck with a poor reader. The cards fall true even for someone who knows nothing about them; you may be able to get a good interpretation just from the cards you see while ignoring the reader's spiel.

The client may also be responsible for blocking the reader. One who has extremely strong defenses or is hostile to the reader may unconsciously cut off all psychic flow. Most experienced readers can deal with this problem by going through some relaxation exercises with the client. Sometimes nothing can be done.

Sometimes the problem is not psychic blocking but a closed mind. Clients who are looking for a specific answer may not want to listen to any other interpretation of the situation--no matter how accurate it is. Readers dread these clients; they tend to return again and again, looking for reassurance, for a new answer, for anything. Again, the client wants something from a reading that the psychic cannot provide.

Good Psychics

Good psychics are knowledgeable, compassionate, skilled, and sensible. They willingly answer questions about their beliefs, techniques, and experience. They are usually willing to have the session taped; many provide tapes at your request. They act as a mirror for your deepest feelings, showing you what you didn't know you knew. They do not always tell you what you want to hear; they tell you the truth as they see it. They are accurate most of the time. They tend to focus less on material occurrences than on spiritual development, less on predictive than on symbolic divination. They gently discourage clients from seeing them too often and from relying on them to make decisions.

Many clients try to test psychics by asking readily verifiable questions. That kind of testing is based on a misapprehension. Being psychic is not the same as being a mind reader. Mind readers are telepaths who can read your thoughts as though they were reading print. Telepathy, by definition, cannot see into the future. A telepath might not necessarily be a good counselor. Incidentally, this is all theoretical; true, full-time telepaths are unbelievably rare.

You are far more likely to meet a reader or psychic. They use their native psychic talents--the ability to sense and interpret another's feelings and the events linked to feelings--along with spiritual or psychic disciplines (such as Tarot or *The Crystal Tree*) to tell you about the present and the future. A good psychic can sense and interpret a person's spiritual and emotional state; look into the future for further developments, opportunities, and choices; sometimes look into the past for roots and causes of problems. Except when an extraordinarily strong psychic contact is made, a reader cannot tell you your parents' names or do other tests. The strong emotion that carries psychic vibrations just isn't there.

A reader may use various tools: cards, crystals, runes; auras, lines on the palm, or tea leaves in the cup; colors, numbers, astrological aspects; the client's personal possessions or simply skin contact. Many can read without tools, but prefer to use cards or crystals because these techniques give their clients something to remember, symbols to remind them of the readings. These tools carry some of the meaning, but the psychic flow determines the interpretations and relationships between the cards or the stones.

If you have specific questions in mind, you should tell the reader what you are concerned about. Be willing to listen to the answer, although sometimes the answer is No or Wait or even Maybe. (An amazing number of people want to hear only Yes, and angrily denounce a reader who says No. These clients drift from reader to reader, searching for the one who will tell them what they want to hear. In the nature of things, they frequently end up with a fraud.) Don't be surprised if some of the things you hear do not fit your preconceived notions; let time pass, and see if they come true. After all, the only final test of a look into the future is the future itself.

Chapter 8

The Wayfarer and the Citizen: Two Pathways to a Fulfilling Life

'Tis time the heart should be unmoved
  Since others it has ceased to move:
Yet, though I cannot be beloved,
  Still let me love! . . .

The fire that on my bosom preys
  Is lone as some volcanic isle;
No torch is kindled at its blaze--
  A funeral pile.

The hope, the fear, the jealous care,
  The exalted portion of the pain
And power of love, I cannot share,
  But wear the chain.
--Lord Byron, "On the Day I Complete
            My Thirty-Sixth Year"

(This is his last poem, found in his diary at Missolonghi; he died less than three months later.)

Man's chief purpose . . . is the creation and preservation of values: that is what gives meaning to our civilization, and the participation in this is what gives significance, ultimately, to the individual human life.

                    --Lewis Mumford, *Faith for Living*

Some people are Wayfarers, whose endless seeking drives them; others are Citizens, whose inner serenity gives them stability.[1] As described here, each is a pure type, but almost no one is entirely one or the other. Most of us blend some Wayfarer attitudes with some Citizen attitudes, depending on time of life or even time of year. In general, though, people seem to be born or initiated early into the characteristic attitude of the Wayfarer or the Citizen.

Both temperaments have characteristic strengths and weaknesses. Both can be valuable and worthwhile ways of living; neither is intrinsically better than the other. Moreover, both temperaments find expression in all faiths, creeds, and ways of life. Some strict traditionalists are Wayfarers, and some of the Citizens subscribe, not to any "traditional" faith, but to Freudianism, New Age thought, or agnosticism. These styles of seeking or maintaining can be applied to anything; some people are resolutely Citizens in their personal relationships but Wayfarers in their work or religion.

It is important to discover where, how, and in what circumstances you respond as a Wayfarer or a Citizen. As you read the descriptions of the Wayfarer and the Citizen, try to imagine yourself as each. If you find yourself violently reacting against one or the other, stop and consider why you are having such a strong reaction. What frightens or repels you? Are you reminded of anyone in your past who acted this way? Who warned you not to act this way? This chapter includes exercises to help you clarify these issues.

THE WAYFARER

The essence of a Wayfarer's life can be seen at a glance; the pursuit of the grail leaves a mark on the seeker, though it is frequently easy--for both an outsider and the Wayfarer--to misjudge what the grail is.

The Wayfarer's strength is a constant awareness of the grail. Whether searching for it through spiritual exercises, physical pleasures, or intellectual researches, Wayfarers always look for the light. Their unslakable hunger and thirst for the truth shapes their lives and may lead them into new insights.

When and if they find a faith, they may not be comfortable in it-- they are temperamentally unlikely to be comfortable for long--but they are likely to be active, tolerant, and compassionate toward others. They understand and can deal with dark nights of the soul, having endured them.

The energy and passion of the Wayfarer are seldom rooted in a strong sense of self-worth; indeed, many Wayfarers suffer from a profound sense of something missing in themselves, a feeling that can range from a healthy desire for God to a deep, unfeigned self-loathing and shame.

Wayfarers, knowing they lack something, seek it endlessly and energetically. They tend to focus their attention so totally on the grail--or on their idea of the grail--that ordinary life loses its savor. Further, if they are unable to identify what they are lacking, they may seek solace in excess. The attempt to quench spiritual thirsts with mental or physical excitements (food, alcohol, drugs, sex, gambling, even books) can end in tragedy, loneliness, and early death. In their raging desire for the grail-- and ultimately for peace--Wayfarers may ruthlessly discard any relationship, idea, or job that does not instantly slake the burning thirst that drives them. Their standards are impossibly high, and they want satisfaction now.

Their single-mindedness may make it difficult to live with Wayfarers; they often have a hard time living with themselves. But they are not simply selfish, overly emotional people, as Citizens may feel. Wayfarers have a vision, a calling, a sense of destiny. The grail within them will not allow them to be still and contented; they must go and find and do. Consequently, they seldom rest on their laurels; they are tireless workers if they are working on their grail. Their spirit of adventure and daring may take them to new realms of knowledge in science, theology, psychology, or history, for example, or to brilliant achievements in the arts. Their extreme and sometimes painful individualism--that will to be themselves--gives them great integrity. Being distanced from the community, they can theorize about it; new political and social developments can often be traced to Wayfarers.

The Wayfarer's characteristic problem is that sheer restlessness may take him or her past the truth and into cynicism; never having found a truth that will satisfy for long, he or she decides there is no truth. At the same time Wayfarers may feel immeasurably superior to those who have accepted tradition, seeing (sometimes correctly) their serenity as complacency.

If the Wayfarer is too frightened and insecure to look for truths beyond the traditional, he or she may project terrors and doubts on those who believe otherwise. The Wayfarer becomes a fanatic determined to burn anyone or anything that threatens the faith, even by disagreeing. The Wayfarer's energy and crusading zeal become instruments of destruction. Because he or she cannot admit to doubts, no one else is permitted to entertain speculations or hold dissenting opinions. The frustrated and frightened Wayfarer becomes more rigid, narrow-minded, and traditionalistic than the most fanatical Citizen.

This portrait of the Wayfarer seems romantic, and it was, in fact, the Wayfarer spirit that drove the romantic poets. George Gordon, Lord Byron, is perhaps the best example of these, for he did ultimately find a grail, but only after tasting every possible substitute. Byron was a notorious sexual profligate (probably, in modern terms, a sex addict; when he was only eight years old he had been molested by his nurse, who alternately beat and preached at him); a vigorous and accomplished athlete (despite his clubfoot) who swam the Hellespont and was famous for his skillful, graceful riding at a time when all gentlemen rode; a poet so famous in his time that he was treated very much as modern rock stars are; and a brilliant, witty conversationalist whose essential sadness and loneliness were perceived only by those very close to him.

Byron's childhood was spent in deep poverty; when Byron was three, his father committed suicide in Paris; at the age of ten, he inherited a title, a heavily mortgaged estate, and a high social position. Passionate and driven by passion, seeking only love and acceptance after his brutal childhood and sudden acquisition of status, he found true love--in the arms of his half-sister, by whom he had a child. He married a cold, analytical woman who was constitutionally unable to understand anyone so driven and difficult; soon, his financial worries and violent temperament made him so impossible to live with that his wife left him, taking their daughter with her. Driven from England, he found solace in debauchery and in his poetry, which had always glorified the Wayfarer--the romantic, restless, unhappy man whose mysterious past and tortured conscience drive him half-mad as he wanders the Earth alone.

But how did such a deeply unhappy man finally find peace? With all his personal passions, Byron also cherished the idea of liberty. He became involved in the movement for Greek independence. He found a cause far greater than himself--the cause of democracy--that also subtly addressed his personal problem of being respected for his title rather than himself, for in a democracy there are no titles. As soon as he became actively involved, his letters and journals changed dramatically: the gloom, cynicism, and self-indulgence gave way to a new spirit of hard work and dedication. He found what he needed--something to do, something to work for. Tragically, the cause killed him; he died in Greece at the age of 36, where he is revered as a martyr to this day.

THE CITIZEN

It is a serious mistake to dismiss Citizens as dull, complacent burghers. They can be warm, loving, and serene, concerned far more with helping and caring for others than with their own pleasures. Because they have a strong foundation, laid early, they need not waste energy exploring dead-end avenues. Instead, they can use their strength in accomplishing their mission, whether that mission is helping the poor and outcast or simply living and working quietly, raising a family, and passing on the tradition of kindness, peace, and goodness. Their strength is in their peace; they can weather crises because they are rooted.

Dull and unimaginative? Not necessarily. A Citizen is too aware of daily life to be dull. There is a savor and a strength to simple, ordinary things that makes Citizens endlessly interesting. They can be visionary, too, but in a quiet way that suits their lives. Visions come to them slowly, thought by thought, and the Citizen is willing to wait until they are complete in every detail. The Citizen's craftsmanship may seem ordinary when it is in process, but the ultimate result is art. The anonymous quilts, pieced and stitched by hand, that now sell for hundreds of thousands of dollars, are an example of the art of the Citizen. Celebratory, joyful, and serene, Citizens make cookies and cathedrals, gardens and governments.

Though there can be drama in the life of the Citizen, it tends to be incidental, not something sought and desired for its own sake. Dramatic or terrible things may happen to a Citizen, but the Citizen is far happier when they are over and he or she can return to real life. But what is real life to a Citizen?

A Citizen's life is a calm, quiet river compared to the stormy seas of the Wayfarer's existence. The Wayfarer may envy its peace and rootedness or despise its apparent passivity and routine. A Citizen's life is usually stable, apparently taken up with quite trivial events. Citizens enjoy traditions: a private calendar of birthdays, annual picnics, and a special breakfast on the first day of school. They cherish their family and their friends.

Living in harmony with the Earth gives Citizens their deep serenity-- a serenity they treasure, often without being consciously aware of it. (Analytical talents are as rare in Citizens as they are in Wayfarers.) Citizens, unlike Wayfarers, are generally both aware of and interested in the world. They see and feel nature deeply and revel in the physicality of life (something a Wayfarer, whose attention is fixed on the grail and his or her own emotions, rarely notices except during moments of sexual pleasure). The seasons pass, each with its own flavor and its particular tasks. A quiet, conscious goodness pervades this life, a goodness of new bread, healthy bodies, pride in craftsmanship, trustworthy friends.

Citizens build. They make homes wherever they go, but they prefer not to go; they would rather stay where they are rooted and understood. A Wayfarer may see this as cowardice or lack of curiosity; a Citizen knows it is courage. It takes a certain kind of strength to go on living where people remember what you did as a child. Citizens cannot run away from that kind of self-knowledge. Consequently, they learn self-acceptance.

In accepting their own faults, they also learn tolerance of others' faults. Citizens are aware of other people, an interest that could be expressed as gossip or as true concern for their neighbors. Citizens live up to their name--they are responsible and they know how to live in community.

Their characteristic problem is complacency. In such an atmosphere of serene acceptance, Citizens may begin to feel proud of not having problems to the point where they can no longer admit that anything is wrong at all, lest the structure of the peaceful world be destroyed. Citizens, being secure, may despise the pain of others, smugly asserting that truly spiritual (or hard-working, or what-have-you) people don't suffer and therefore those who suffer deserve what they get. They may (sometimes correctly) dismiss the Wayfarer's quest as evidence of instability or thrill-seeking. Moreover, since the Citizen seldom questions authority or even him/herself, he or she may be devastated by an unexpected crisis of faith when a respected spiritual leader falls or when tragedy strikes.

A portrait of an archetypal Citizen is harder to find than one of an archetypal Wayfarer because Wayfarers, in their searches, more often stumble on fame than do Citizens. However, there is one Citizen whose life history has been rendered with great finesse and delicacy of detail and who is familiar to many: Frodo, the Hobbit in J. R. R. Tolkien's *Lord of the Rings* trilogy. Anyone who has read the Tolkien books will have an immediate and vivid idea of the delights of a Citizen's life. (For some reason English novelists have a far greater respect for the Citizen's life than do Americans. Perhaps Americans prize restlessness because we would not be here if our ancestors had remained peacefully at home.) Kenneth Grahame also evoked the pleasures of being a Citizen in *The Wind in the Willows*. The extraordinary chapter titled "Dolce Domum" ("home, sweet home") is the ultimate expression of a Citizen's reverence for home.

Being a Citizen, however, is not all Middle Earth, any more than a Wayfarer's life is all Byron and bourbon. Some Citizens change the world. Mother Teresa of Calcutta embodies the best traits of the Citizen: deep concern and love for her neighbors and a warm and down-to-Earth serenity that manages to be both practical and spiritual. Though she left her native country of Albania, she has never left the faith with which she grew up. Her secret is that she acts on what she believes and she depends on the Lord. She has never sought publicity. She has simply done what was needed, what came next. Her humility, simplicity, and peace are not deceptive or put on; she could not do what she does without that inner strength.

WAYFARER OR CITIZEN?

The questions below, like all the questions in this book, are steps in the path through the labyrinth, where you can go only forward into self-knowledge--or backward. Answer them honestly as you are now, not as you would like to be. Only the truth will set you free.

Some qualities of the Wayfarer and the Citizen are laid out in Table 8.1.

In general, are you more a Wayfarer or more a Citizen? _____

Has this always been true? _____

If yes, when did you first become aware of what you were like? _____

_____

_____

_____

If no, when and how did you begin to change? _____

_____

_____

_____

If you could choose three Wayfarer qualities, what would they be?

_____

_____

_____

Write down a way you can encourage the latent Wayfarer qualities you admire. _____

_____

_____

If you could choose three Citizen qualities, what would they be? _____

_____

_____

_____

Write down a way you can encourage the latent Citizen qualities you admire. _____

_____

_____

_____

Table 8.1: The Wayfarer and the Citizen

Wayfarer	*Citizen*
mutable	fixed
restless	at peace
yearning	fulfilled
unstable	unchanging
innovator	preserver
makes discoveries	keeps traditions
doubting	sure
wandering	rooted
searching	sustaining
free	secure
pursues	possesses
eager	steadfast
driven by desire	held still by contentment
the road	the home
to do	to be
the fire of heaven	the salt of the Earth
individualistic	communitarian
aware of self	aware of others
art	craftsmanship
intransigent	adaptable

Fill out the following chart of your Wayfarer and Citizen qualities. (These proportions will almost certainly change as you move through different stages of life.)

In my inner self, I am _____% Wayfarer and _____% Citizen.

In my private mythology, I am _____% Wayfarer and _____% Citizen.

At work, I am _____% Wayfarer and _____% Citizen.

With possessions, I am _____% Wayfarer and _____% Citizen.

In my attitude toward nature, I am _____% Wayfarer and _____% Citizen.

Intellectually, I am _____% Wayfarer and _____% Citizen.

When making changes, I am _____% Wayfarer and _____% Citizen.

In friendships, I am _____% Wayfarer and _____% Citizen.

In romantic relationships, I am _____% Wayfarer and _____% Citizen.

With my family, I am _____% Wayfarer and _____% Citizen.

Emotionally, I am _____% Wayfarer and _____% Citizen.

Spiritually, I am _____% Wayfarer and _____% Citizen.

Exercises

In the following exercises, you will be following your Wayfarer and Citizen selves into their separate worlds. You will probably find it easier to do the exercises separately; the life of a Wayfarer may seem lonely and dangerous after a satisfying vision of the Citizen self, or the Citizen life may seem tame and unadventurous after a wild expedition into the Wayfarer life. Unless you are a writer yourself--perhaps even if you are!--you may find it easier to do the visualization first and then write it in your journal. Most people find that a pen in the hand paralyzes every thought in the brain, and these visualizations are best, most meaningful, and most fun when you feel free to play with them. But do write down the salient points of your daydream because you will need them later!

Visualization: The Wayfarer

Visualize yourself as a Wayfarer. You may imagine yourself in any period of history, in either gender, doing whatever you desire. Let the visualization become clear and vivid and accurate. If, for example, you cannot bear hot weather, your visualization of yourself as a jungle explorer will be unrealistic. Though we are not sticking to the merely possible here, we are looking for the probable as we work outward from the central and essential core of selfhood. By the same token, do not limit yourself too much. You need not be bound by custom or by what you have not yet learned. If the Wayfarer of your dreams rides a powerful black stallion, you need not know how to ride.

Let yourself dream about every aspect of the Wayfarer life.

--In what ways would your life change?

--What would you do that you are not doing now?

--Would you look different or dress differently?

--What kind of work would you be doing?

--Where and how would you live?

--Who would be with you, and what would your relationships be like?

--What would your sexual relationships be like?

--Would you have children?

--How would you deal with anger, sorrow, pain, loneliness?

--How would you deal with peace, joy, pleasure?

--What would you do in your spare time?

--The most important question comes last: What would be your central, driving quest if you were a Wayfarer, and how would you pursue it?

Journal: The Wayfarer

Write down the Wayfarer fantasy, paying special attention to the questions asked. You may want to write in story form rather than as a series of answers to the questions, or you may want to do it as an essay.

Later--an hour, a day, a week--go back to your fantasy. Redream it if you want, and look at what you wrote in your notebook. Then think about what you like best in your Wayfarer life.

--Are there elements you can incorporate into your life now?

--Is your Wayfarer self getting enough room, enough air, enough expression in the way you live now?

--Are there specific activities--fencing, horseback riding, long solitary walks--that you can do as a Wayfarer?

--Can you be more daring and original in the way you dress, the music you listen to, the friends you make?

--Does your Wayfarer crave a solitude that you deny yourself?

In your journal, write down the different ways you might express your Wayfarer self. If you feel self-conscious, write that down, too, but don't let it stop you from making the experiment. If your Wayfarer self writes poetry, you can turn your hand to writing some. It doesn't have to be Shakespeare to be an honest expression of yourself. (If you find writing poetry unsatisfying, you might try reading some. It can give your life an unexpected incandescence.) Try on different aspects of your Wayfarer self, one or two changes at a time--a new hairstyle, a more adventurous attitude. If one element proves less exciting, romantic, or pleasant than you had imagined, write that down and move on to the next experiment. You owe it to yourself--and to God--to be all you were meant to be.

Visualization: The Citizen

Visualize yourself as a Citizen. You may imagine yourself in any period of history, in either gender, doing whatever you desire. Let the visualization become clear and vivid and accurate. Again, be honest with yourself about what is physically and emotionally possible for you. The Citizen is still you; fantasies unconnected with your true self can never reveal areas of yourself that can develop and grow.

Let yourself dream about every aspect of the Citizen life.

--In what ways would your life change?

--What would you do that you are not doing now?

--Would you look different or dress differently?

--What kind of work would you be doing?

--Where and how would you live?

--Who would be with you, and what would your relationships be like?

--What would your sexual relationships be like?

--Would you have children?

--How would you deal with anger, sorrow, pain, loneliness?

--How would you deal with peace, joy, pleasure?

--What would you do in your spare time?

--The most important question comes last: What would be the central source of your serenity and peace if you were a Citizen, and how would you express it?

Journal: The Citizen

Write down the Citizen fantasy, paying special attention to the questions asked. You may want to write in story form rather than as a series of answers to the questions, or you may want to do it as an essay.

Later--an hour, a day, a week--go back to your fantasy. Redream it if you want, and look at what you wrote in your notebook. Then think about what you like best in your Citizen life.

--Are there elements you can incorporate into your life now?

--Is your Citizen self getting enough room, enough air, enough expression in the way you live now?

--Are there specific activities--gardening, bread-baking, playing with children--that you can do as a Citizen?

--Can you be more in touch with the natural world, with your family, with social issues?

--Are you looking for work that gives you pride and satisfaction, not just a paycheck?

--Can you find an inner core of serenity and strength in the music you listen to, your friends, your family?

--Does your Citizen crave social and family involvement that you deny yourself?

In your journal, write down the different ways you might express your Citizen self. If you feel self-conscious, write that down, too, but don't let it stop you from making the experiment. If your Citizen self refinishes old furniture, you can turn your hand to that skill. You don't have to begin by redoing a treasured and priceless antique; you can start by practicing on an inexpensive piece from a yard sale or thrift shop. There is a deep joy in craftsmanship that our prepackaged culture misses. Like poetry, craftsmanship can make your life glow. Try one or two changes at a time--bake bread or muffins from scratch, buy a philodendron for your window and care for it. That philodendron may be enough, or it may lead you to bigger gardens or a farm. The point is to start somewhere. If one element proves less satisfying than you had imagined, write that down and move on to the next experiment. You owe it to yourself--and to God--to be all you were meant to be.

NOTE

1. In codifying this deep distinction between ways of living, I found it unexpectedly difficult to find positive words for the Citizen. Stay-at-

homes, sticks-in-the-mud, leftovers, reactionaries, the unadventurous, the dull, the unmoving--these were the kinds of words, with their freight of scornful connotations, that I found for those who keep the hearth and civilization going. We tend to despise people who stay in the same place, as though keeping and maintaining were lesser accomplishments than moving. This attitude may be part of American culture's contempt for the old-fashioned and adulation of the new; it may also be additional evidence of the pervasive misogyny of our culture, since women have traditionally kept the hearth while men went adventuring. It may be unnecessary to emphasize that I believe both modes of living are essential to a balanced and happy life; you must be able both to go off on quests and stay home and cultivate your own garden.

Chapter 9

The Eyes of Heaven: Finding a Spiritual Perspective

You would not seek Him if you had not already found Him.
--Blaise Pascal, *Pensées*

Meditation is not a means to an end. It is both the means and the end.

--Krishnamurti

Don't wait for the Last Judgment. It takes place every day.
--Albert Camus, *The Fall*

What doth the Lord require of thee, but to do justly, and to love mercy, and to walk humbly with thy God?

--Micah 6:8

So far, we have dealt with the quest in secular terms: as a process of self-discovery and self-actualization; of discovering karma and destiny; or, to put the process in its simplest possible form, as a kind of awakening process whereby you become aware of both yourself and the world. Having begun to see yourself and the world, you can now look beyond it to the realm of the spirit.

The spiritual dimension of life is the ultimate and most important part of ourselves. Indeed, it is not a part in the sense that it can be divided from the rest of the person. Self-discovery--even of minor tastes and pleasures, even of the Shadow--is a spiritual journey. At some point you must deal with what you believe. At some point you must face God.

All along you have been awakening or energizing the spiritual perspective in you. The grail quest is ultimately a search for the meaning of life, and there is no meaning of life without the spirit. Whatever your faith, whatever your beliefs, to be whole you must discover the spiritual perspective: the eyes of heaven.

Seeing things in a spiritual perspective requires exercises, but not the kind we have done all through the book. The first and foremost exercise is prayer, then the quest for God, and then what I have called the "eyes of heaven": a new way of looking at everything.

SOME NOTES ON PRAYER

Why Pray?

Virtually no one attains peace and enlightenment without regular prayer. In prayer we speak to God and listen for an answer. No other spiritual technique can get us closer to God. The ongoing dialogue of prayer offers us the chance to meditate and clear our minds; to confess our lapses and be forgiven; to praise and worship God; to thank God; to ask for our daily bread; to plead for guidance, wisdom, and the health and strength of others; to simply talk with God in a kind of pure conversation that cannot be described, only experienced.

Why is prayer commanded by every religion? It provides a deep connection with the spiritual that feeds us and blesses us. It is a way for goodness to come into our lives. It even offers physiological benefits. Ultimately, we pray because it is intrinsically good to pray, not because it offers the same benefits as aerobic exercise without all the sweat.

Meditation, especially, calms and soothes. Its physical effects are now common knowledge: It lowers the blood pressure and keeps us healthy. Meditation cleanses as well; its concentrated peace, stillness, and serenity act like a brief vacation. Ten minutes of meditation can rest you more than an hour of sleep. Yet I am uncomfortable advertising meditation as merely a mid-afternoon boost for tired muscles; somehow it cheapens the real meaning of the renewal and refreshment it provides. Meditation enables you to see the mundane world through spiritual eyes. It enriches your sense of the world as a created place filled with meaning and pattern. It can help you be kinder to your neighbor and more faithful to God.

Confession in prayer to God also changes the way you see the world. Admitting your faults and lapses promotes humility and eases your conscience; as any psychotherapist can tell you, it is far better to tell what you have done (and what has been done to you) than to let it fester inside. The humiliation of confession, painful as it is, also affords the release of forgiveness. Once confessed, your faults can be seen in proper perspective--neither meaningless nor Earth-shaking, but normal, human, and forgivable while at the same time being potentially painful and destructive.

You may also be interested in confessing any hurts and pain you have suffered during the day and your reactions to them. For example, if a friend has been rude and unfeeling to you, "confess" it and confess your own reaction as well. Did you sulk, snap back, make light of it? Are you willing to forgive others? Praying about difficult events can give you a new perspective on them. If you need to confront your friend about repeated rudenesses, prayer can show you kind and loving ways to do so. If your friend was simply thoughtless, perhaps no action is called for--just forgive and forget. In either case, prayer shows you the path to take.

Praising God and offering worship are easily confused with one another; indeed, they frequently overlap. Praise is recognizing and rejoicing in God's qualities: glory, majesty, justice, love, power, and so on. Worship is a personal commitment to honor and adore the God who displays those qualities. Why praise? Why worship? So far as I know, neither one specifically lowers your blood pressure or gives the sense of freedom of a thorough confession. Yet they promote intimacy with God. Just as you are closer to your mate (or your children or your friends) when you praise one another and offer love and commitment, so you are closer to God when you offer praise and worship. Not everything demands an instant return. We must not think of a relationship with God as being a mercantile contract, in which we give two hours of prayer and praise per week in exchange for favors granted. If you conduct your relationships on that heartless and calculating level, they will soon be empty and meaningless; so will your relationship with God, Who is not interested in bargains.

Praise and worship show commitment, and it is commitment that is at issue here. No prayer can be meaningful without commitment; no marriage can survive long without a deep commitment of two people to each other. God is always willing; are you? Do you, can you, commit yourself freely and fully to God? Through giving yourself unreservedly in prayer, you will be blessed with more faith and more ability to give yourself unreservedly. If you cannot give yourself at all, there is no point to prayer (or, for that matter, to anything else in this book, which is predicated on the idea that existence has a meaning provided by God and discoverable by ourselves). That spiritual commitment can become the shining beacon in your life, and praise and worship may come to express the deepest feelings of your soul.

Thanksgiving also builds closeness to God. Few prayers are more simple, more sincere, or more blessed than the spontaneous prayer of thanks for the beauty of the day or of a child, but more formal thanks are also in order. Offer thanks for food to eat, clothes to wear, a roof over your head, a job to work at; for friends, family, mate, and children; for chances to help others and for the help others give you; for anything that rejoices your soul or rests your bones. Perhaps this sounds dry, stilted, childish. But remember the help prayer gives when you discuss daily problems and troubles with God. The joy of sharing all the blessings of life and thanking God for them deepens the happiness you feel.

Asking for daily bread and other necessities is allied to thanksgiving; in doing so, you acknowledge the source of all that is good in life. Some people find it humiliating to ask; they may point out that they have tomorrow's food stored in the freezer and thus they need not ask for it. Yet it still belongs to God, and it is only polite to ask. Furthermore, you never know; you may count on tomorrow's food while not counting on natural or human-made disasters.

Asking for guidance, wisdom, and self-knowledge and praying for others are somewhat different than the request for daily bread. Praying for spiritual gifts for yourself may be the only way to obtain them. Praying for someone else who is ill, in trouble, or in need demonstrates the deepest love and concern you can offer. Though the sick may not be healed, they will be given strength--and often, during such prayers, God reveals how the petitioner him- or herself can be the instrument of helping the person prayed for. Do not ignore such calls! There is no point in praying for someone whom you cannot be bothered to help in person; that attitude demonstrates insincerity and lack of commitment.

The ongoing conversation with God is a high form of prayer. In addition to saying formal prayers, you can talk constantly to God--to pray without ceasing. Thus the spontaneous praise or thanks, the quick word of supplication for patience or for peace, the repeated ritual prayer, colors your thoughts as you work, drive, exercise, eat, and do all the other tasks of daily life. This is the spiritual life as it is meant to be: not in addition to or separate from "real life," but woven into the fabric of real life itself, so that life without prayer would be as unthinkable as life without breath.

What Is Prayer?

Praying may consist of repeating set ritual prayers aloud or silently; meditation and contemplation with or without such aids to attention as mantras, statues, icons, candles, music, and incense; or spontaneous dialogues (silent or spoken) with God, thanking, praising, questioning, petitioning, or confessing to the Supreme Being. There are other ways to pray, but these are the primary ones used in our culture.

Ritual Prayers

Ritual prayers satisfy the human need for structure and familiarity. Some religious sects rely heavily on ritual prayers and blessings, while others rely less on ceremonial and more on spontaneous prayers. (It must be noted, however, that sects that make little use of ritual prayers tend to use repeated and almost ritual quotations from the holy scriptures instead.)

When reciting ritual prayers alone or in a group, the worshiper feels like part of a great tradition; shared prayers can unite people from many different countries and cultures. Once memorized, they can be repeated without conscious thought, giving the effect of a mantra. When prayed consciously or made the subject of a meditation, they generally offer up rich treasures of spiritual meaning.

The familiar prayers of childhood can also give the individual a sense of continuity and personal significance. Your personal history adds a depth of meaning to the ritual. What can mean more to you than the prayers you prayed all your life--prayers that comforted you in times of stress, loss, loneliness; that expressed your joy and exultation; prayers that may have been part of your childhood, your wedding, your grieving for the deaths of loved ones, your own children's lives; and that will comfort others when you eventually die?

Yet ritual prayers are sometimes criticized as not being spontaneous, personal, or sincere. Certainly they are not spontaneous, but ritual prayer does not preclude spontaneous prayer. Ideally the two should be balanced in your life. Whether they are "personal" and "sincere" depends entirely on the attitude of the person who is praying. Even the most apparently spontaneous and sincere prayer may be mere public speaking if the worshiper's heart is not in it. If you find the ritual prayers of your faith empty of meaning, perhaps you are repeating them in a routine fashion; perhaps you are withholding yourself unconsciously; perhaps you no longer believe; perhaps you are simply going through a dry spell, in which nothing much seems to have significance. In any case, if your ritual prayers are dry, are your spontaneous prayers any more meaningful? If they are, perhaps you are in the wrong tradition of worship. If they, too, are dry and apparently meaningless, you should seek guidance from a clergyperson or another more experienced person of your faith.

Meditation and Contemplation

Meditation and contemplation are similar to each other but somewhat unlike other kinds of prayer. Both are receptive rather than active--that is, in either you wait, listen, and accept rather than ask, tell, or give. Meditation opens you to the speaking of God; contemplation opens you to thoughts about the spiritual, which lead to closeness to God. Meditation seeks God's thoughts; contemplation helps us find our own. Meditation may be *focused by* outside stimuli (from music to incense), but it is not *focused on* the stimulus, as contemplation is. Meditation is a way of listening for the music of heaven. Contemplation is a way of viewing an object or an idea in the light of heaven.

An example may make this distinction (which I admit is a fine one, not usually drawn) a little clearer. If Joan wants to meditate, she goes about the process that Quakers call "centering down," a way of relaxing the conscious mind. By gradually clearing herself of mundane preoccupations, she opens the way for God to speak. In order to help herself clear her mind, she may get into a yoga position, play soft and undistracting music on the stereo (or if she is home with her noisy family, put on headphones), burn incense, go into an empty church or mosque or synagogue, close her eyes, or follow a tea ritual. Any or all of these techniques help mark the difference from Joan's ordinary activities and her meditation. None is the *subject* of her meditation; she does not think about the incense, the music, or the tea. They merely help her redirect her energies and create an atmosphere conducive to meditation.

If Joan wants to do contemplation, however, she might (or might not) make similar preparations. She would, however, choose something to be the subject of her contemplation. She may, perhaps, pick the scent of the incense, a statue or painting or natural scene, a word or idea or attribute of God, or a piece of music. Good contemplation can be done when doing almost anything. There is a lovely and meaningful contemplation on cutting up an onion in Robert Farrar Capon's *The Supper of the Lamb*. Once you have made something the subject of your contemplation, you may never see it in quite the same way again. It will always have the faint, bright edge of the holy upon it.

Spontaneous Prayers

No one can teach you to pray spontaneously, for spontaneous prayer is an open expression of the feelings of your heart addressed to God. In sharing everything with the Spirit, you will gain a new sweetness and balance. When your mind and heart are filled with prayer, how can you be cruel, petty, or selfish? The continuous dialogue with the Spirit shapes your thoughts, actions, and emotions.

THE QUEST FOR GOD

If you have already "found" God--if you have a deep personal faith--you know that finding God is not like finding a penny, which you can drop in your piggy bank and forget. Finding God entails a lifelong search for deeper truths, a clearer understanding of the mystery and majesty of God. It is not something done once and finished; it is a process of meeting, learning, growing, and changing. The Almighty is so much greater and more complex than we can imagine that there is always more to learn and more to love. New insights and new tests of faith keep coming.

If you have not found God, I can promise this: The earnest seeker will find God. If you are willing to believe, God will help you. But how does one hunt for God? Prayer is the first step. Then read the Bible and other spiritual books. Talk to those who have searched and found. Keep asking. Keep looking. In mythology, in some of the world's great fiction, in music, the secret is hidden.[1]

THE EYES OF HEAVEN

A spiritual perspective can be seen as just that: perspective, seeing things at the right distance and in the right light. A recurring symbol in the literature of spirituality is the single eye. Odin, who hung nine nights on the sacred tree, gave one eye to obtain wisdom. Jesus said that having a single eye would fill our bodies with light--would make our earthly existence like heaven. But how can you have perspective (which requires two eyes, to give perception of depth) with only one eye?

Those who have two eyes see from their own viewpoint only. (We are speaking metaphorically here, though the metaphor is based on anatomy. Please don't put out your eye in order to become spiritual, as a few misguided fictional characters have done.) The sacrifice of one eye is not a loss of vision; the dead eye is resurrected as a spiritual eye. That is the perspective of heaven: to be able to see on human terms as well as in God's terms.

An example may illuminate this rather unusual concept. Margaret, the woman who had been an abused child, at first could not admit that her experience was out of the normal range. It was too painful for her to see it at all. She had her eyes shut. When she opened her eyes, she saw only with a human perspective. She saw the damage that had been done to her, and she was grieved and enraged. (Some people stay in that state for all their lives; they never gain perspective on what has happened to them, and they therefore never can forgive and forget. The sight of their sufferings is always in their eyes, and they cannot recover from it. Indeed, they frequently pass it on to the next generation.) But Margaret went on to obtain a spiritual perspective. She learned to see the pain her own parents had suffered when they were children. She learned to see both the effect and the intent. Therefore, she could forgive. She saw as God sees. That is a spiritual perspective.

The spiritual perspective is not limited to ways of looking at your own past or at the actions of others. It is a way of looking at every action and thought and idea, not just for your own immediate gain or advantage, but from the viewpoint of heaven. The spiritual perspective can influence your choice of career. Would anyone illegally dump toxic waste, sell drugs, or become a corporate raider if they had the spiritual perspective? No. People do those things for money or glory, thinking only of their worldly success and position, not of the consequences in terms of public health or crack babies or bankrupted companies and unemployed workers. In other words they have their eye on the main chance, not on the spiritual meaning of their work.

The quest demands a coherent life--a life that is whole, significant, meaningful, real. Factory work can be meaningful if you deeply believe in the product and if you believe that your labor has significance. The choice of how you live (simply or grandly or in between), what you value, and whom you love and like are all essentially and ultimately spiritual issues. If life is significant, if your actions matter, if you have dignity as a human being, then so does everyone else. They all deserve to be treated humanly. You cannot be bigoted or cruel. You cannot dismiss the consequences of any action. You cannot live an unexamined life. If you are going on a quest, you must be responsible to that quest. You must make the commitment to look at the world with the eyes of heaven, to live responsibly, to make your life as whole and meaningful and coherent and beautiful as the created Universe that you mirror.

NOTE

1. But what is the story that can save us? What is the story mythology tells over and over?

The god of light who dies in spring dies on a tree in order to bring forgiveness and wisdom and holiness and blessings to his people. Sometimes he is symbolically resurrected. Once he was really resurrected. We have made no new myths since then; tales and legends and stories, yes, and histories as well, but no new myths. Their richness and meaning once intersected with history; the shining power of significance and meaning once was embodied in a living, sweating, loving human person, not imperfectly embodied (for we all have a touch of the mythological about us), but fully embodied. God was a man for a while. Then he died in a way unimaginably cruel; he went into the Shadow, he went into hell. But he came back.

That resurrection is mirrored in a minor way in the symbolic resurrections of mythic gods whose rites are forgotten or remembered only by archaeologists. It is mirrored in our own death-and-resurrection experiences, in which we are changed utterly but remain the same; by facing the Shadow in ourselves and coming out the other side. Remember the basic principle of metaphysics: "As above, so below." The passion and resurrection of the Christ is reflected by the death and rebirth of the year, of all things. Remember the cycle of balance and change--that is the cycle of death and resurrection. Because it has happened for real, it need never be done again.

You can find God in this story. You can find faith. Here is the one person who can assure you of meaning in life, of forgiveness, of peace. Believe that once myth was embodied--that the imagined and pretended and lesser sacrifices once culminated in the ultimate sacrifice--and that now you need only give yourself in full commitment to the One who died. All of Earth--all the natural cycles, the hidden and magnificent complexities of life--point to this single truth. Everything in the created Universe reflects the mind of the maker. That central drama of our sins, His suffering and death and resurrection, and our ability to accept or reject the sacrifice is the central drama of all mythology.

Chapter 10

Keys to Your Destiny

But at my back I always hear
Time's winged chariot hurrying near. . . .
Let us roll all our strength and all
Our sweetness up into one ball
And tear our pleasures with rough strife
Thorough the iron gates of life.
 --Andrew Marvell, "To His Coy Mistress"

The Present is the point at which time touches eternity. Of the present moment, and of it only, humans have an experience analogous to the experience which [God] has of reality as a whole; in it alone freedom and actuality are offered them.
 --C.S. Lewis, *The Screwtape Letters*

Try not to become a man of success, but a man of value.
 --Albert Einstein

Only connect! That was the whole of her sermon. Only connect the prose and the passion, and both will be exalted, and human love will be seen at its height. Live in fragments no longer.

 --E.M. Forster, *Howard's End*

Whether you believe in reincarnation, in heaven, or in no afterlife at all, one fact is evident: The only time you have to live (and prepare for your afterlife) is now. You may have been reincarnated a thousand times--as every famous person from Cleopatra to King George III--but you cannot relive those lives. Nor can you choose to deal with an issue or fulfill your destiny in your next life; how do you know you'll have a chance?

Because the past is unchangeable and the future uncertain, the present is crucial. If this life is all you have, every choice may decide your destiny; the present moment suddenly becomes holy and irreplaceable.

This chapter will not tell you about past lives.[1] It will, instead, teach you some ways to find the patterns and meanings of your present life-- the one that seems alternately dull and frightening, with occasional flashes of pure joy.

WHAT SHOULD I DO?: THE QUESTION OF DESTINY

The process of finding your destiny has already begun. Throughout this book you have been looking at the raw materials of the self: Who you are and what you like, love, hate, and fear; what you want to spend your time doing; what you already have struggled with; what you are good at doing. None of the discoveries came by chance.

You were not chosen by lot to perform your destiny, you were created to fulfill it. *Fulfill* has two shades of meaning, as different as the implications of *finish* and *complete*. Fulfill--in its sense of finishing-- means to achieve, to reach your goal. It is a view that considers only the purpose or end, not the means. That's a black-and-white, pass-fail, binary view. Failure or success is judged solely by results. This is the ordinary way of looking at success.

But *fulfill* has another meaning, one closely linked to *fulfillment* (a sense of satisfaction, of having found a place and a task for oneself). In its sense of completion, fulfill means to carry out a mission, satisfy a requirement, serve a purpose. You embody your destiny; in completing your task, you make yourself whole. This view considers your life as a gestalt: the process and structure of all you do; the texture of your daily life; the integration of your destiny with your ordinary obligations to other people, with your pleasures, with the way you think. Your destiny is more than a trophy brought back from a cosmic scavenger hunt. *How* you try to get it is actually more important than whether, in fact, you succeed. The means justify the end.

Conventional marks of success--large houses and cars, your name in the headlines, fan letters from strangers--are irrelevant to fulfilling your destiny. You can easily fulfill your destiny and not become rich and famous; that's the pattern most people follow. Others become famous only after they are dead: Vincent van Gogh, whose paintings now sell for tens of millions of dollars, sold one painting in his life. A few get rich for other, incidental reasons; only a tiny percentage (impossible to determine) actually win fame and fortune to fulfill their destiny. It doesn't matter either way. Success is not the point--fulfillment is.

Your destiny is unique to you, because it is more than a single set task that you must perform. It is a complex puzzle--a maze--that includes personal relationships, self-healing, accomplishments at work, spiritual attitudes, and a thousand other factors. The invisible effect you have on others is just as important as the achievements you're aware of and proud of. Your destiny is a process of developing your soul. If you turn willfully aside from it, what are you doing but crippling a soul?

Spiritual development goes on whether you're aware of it or not, in ordinary tasks as well as in meditation and prayer. The quest was designed to help you become aware of yourself so you could discover where and how to go in order to create a whole self, live a complete life, and thus fulfill your destiny.

Some Misconceptions

Your destiny is not a station on a single-track railroad, a place you must reach if you go forward at all. It is the center of a labyrinth, a labyrinth that (once you can safely look back from the center) is constructed on the principle of whatever lessons you needed to learn to be able to perform the task in the center of the maze. The design is, in fact, karma.

The maze image has one drawback: It may reinforce the common misconception that if you have a mission, you have one single mission to and for which you should sacrifice everything else. Nothing should stand in the way of your destiny--not friends, family, rose gardens, music, anything. But that attitude is destructive and wrong. Your destiny is not the single issue on which you'll be judged, and you have many missions --some of greater importance--all at the same time. As you grow older, you'll finish some early ones and start new ones. You are not a machine designed to fulfill one function and then be discarded.

Work and Destiny

Your job is not necessarily your destiny, although it can be a part of it. The right job can help create the complete life. The process of coming to know yourself, which will help you understand your destiny, can help you understand what kind of job is best for you. The same techniques can be used to help you make other choices: where to live, ways to change, and so on.

To help you understand your relationships--with lovers, family, friends, co-workers--you can do the exercises with someone else. Sharing these truths about yourself can create new intimacy and provide unexpected rewards. More details will be given in the section on interpreting the results.

DETERMINING YOUR DESTINY: EXERCISES

1. What Are You Like?

These exercises will help you distill the self-knowledge gained in the exercises throughout the book (especially in Chapter 3). Even at this late point, you may feel foolish telling yourself what you like and dislike, but how often do you really consult your own tastes and wishes? It's far more likely that you do what's convenient, expected, or fashionable. Answer honestly; concealing the truth cheats only yourself. These exercises can be repeated annually to reflect your growth and change or whenever facing a new beginning.

Crystal Exercise

Choose three stones from a group of stones and crystals. The first represents your personality, the second your motivations, the third your way of self-expression. For interpretations, see Table 10.1.

Stone 1 _____

Stone 2 _____

Stone 3 _____

Visualizing

Imagine yourself doing something you enjoy. Is it active or quiet? Are you alone or with others? If you're with others, are you competing or working together?

Journal Exercise

Write a dialogue with yourself. Tell yourself what you like, want, enjoy. If you like something and are afraid of it--whether it's sex, rock music, psychic work, or whatever--write a dialogue between the part of yourself that likes the forbidden activity and the part of yourself that fears it.

Music Exercise

Discover what your five favorite pieces of music are. These will change over time, so you should think carefully about what you like best now. Listen to them all--not necessarily in one session--and think about why you like them and how they make you feel.

Art Exercise

Draw, sculpt, paint, or embroider a self-portrait. It can be symbolic or representational.

2. What Are Your Best Choices?

These exercises help you find the best choices for your life. The crystal exercise indicates the nature of your talents; the others help you find which directions may be best for you. By imagining yourself in other situations, you learn which choices are wrong before you invest your time and energy in them. For those who want specific career counseling, there are professional tests to measure levels of skill, talent, or creativity. These are listed in the Further References.

Crystal Exercise

Choose three stones from a group of stones and crystals. The first represents your chief talent, the second your creativity, the third your way of expressing yourself. For interpretations, see Table 10.1.

Stone 1 _____

Stone 2 _____

Stone 3 _____

Visualizing

Imagine what daily life is like in different fields or professions that you're interested in. Be honest and think logically. If you're thinking of being a reporter, for example, don't just think of interviewing celebrities and getting a byline. Think of tight deadlines, writing about events that may upset you, and having to read the newspaper every day.

Journal Exercise

Think back to three important choices in your life. Write a story about what would have happened if you had chosen differently in each case. How would you be different? Would you be happier or less happy? If you feel you made the wrong choice, think about ways to change the consequences of your choice. What have you learned from the choices you made?

3. What Are the Patterns of Your Life?

These exercises are designed to help you discover the meaning in the apparently random events of your life. In order to do so, you must first remember the events and feelings--remember them honestly and think about their meanings. Then you must look for the patterns, using both analytical and metaphorical thinking. The process itself may be painful; if you have had a very difficult life, you may want to go through these exercises with a counselor.

Crystal Exercise

Choose three stones from a group of stones and crystals. The first represents your early life, the second your current life, the third your possibilities for later life. For interpretations, see Table 10.1.

Stone 1 _____

Stone 2 _____

Stone 3 _____

Visualizing

Remember the three best times in your life. What made them so good? Could you recapture that feeling and use it in other ways? Remember the three worst times. Why were they so bad? Could you have done anything to improve them? What did you learn from them?

Journal Exercise

Write your autobiography, focusing on the one area of life that has given you the most trouble (relationships, possessions, family, whatever). You may want to try this using several different viewpoints.

Art Exercise

Draw, paint, model, or otherwise express how you felt at the best and worst times of your life.

Metaphor Game

Come up with as many metaphors for the pattern of your life as you can. For example, your life might be a spiderweb, a train station, a thundery August afternoon, an unfinished painting, an adventure movie, and a lost cat wandering through strange forests.

4. What Stands in Your Way?

These exercises are designed to help you identify and remove or diminish some of the walls, blocks, and obstacles--psychological, emotional, and spiritual barriers to growth and change.

Crystal Exercise

Choose three stones from a group of stones and crystals. The first represents your chief stumbling block, the second an unconscious block, the third a block involving family or relationships. For interpretations, see Table 10.1.

Stone 1 _____

Stone 2 _____

Stone 3 _____

Visualizing

Imagine your frustrations, blocks, and problems as a wall. What shape and color is it? Who built it? What is it made of? Talk to it and listen to it talk back. Whose voice does it have?

Journal Exercise

List what stands in your way and think of twenty ways to get around it. Don't censor your list, just write as fast as possible. Even if something seems to be nonsense, write it down. Later, you will go back and interpret.

Art Exercise

Draw, paint, model, or otherwise express all that prevents you from doing what you want to, and then express ways to conquer those blocks.

Metaphor Game

Come up with as many metaphors for the obstacles in your way as you can. For example, they might be a wall, a lid on a box (with you inside), a long wait in line, a flat tire, a lion in your way. Then match ways of dealing with the obstacle to each metaphor. You might climb the wall or build a staircase to the top, saw a hole in the lid and climb out, read or meditate while you wait in line, fix the flat tire or learn to hitchhike, and make a friend of the lion.

5. Is This Worthy of an Immortal Being?

If you suddenly realized that you were immortal, you would begin to see that the choices you make now will be reflected not just for a day or a year but for eternity. You would start asking yourself if what you were doing with your life is worthy of an immortal soul. You would change your life to reflect that new vision of yourself--the white flame noble in you, lasting forever, created by a loving God for a specific purpose--and answerable for the way it expressed itself in life.

That urgency, freshness, and passion are the ways we are supposed to live. Your choice of work, your relationships with other people, your willingness to learn and grow and change and forgive, your attitude toward the created Universe and toward the Creator--all are transformed by the realization that what you do matters. Every second matters. Certain questions become urgent: How do your choices look, not in the light of the next day or week or lifetime, but in the light of eternity? Are you *now* living in a way that befits an immortal? You are an immortal soul. What you do matters. Stop dreaming of your years as a gold prospector or a harem slave in the seraglio of Topkapi. The years that matter are the ones passing now; they are the only ones you can change.

These exercises are designed to help you see yourself in the clear light of eternity.

Visualizing

Imagine your destiny--and your ordinary life--in the light of spiritual values. What is the holy thing to do? Imagine yourself explaining your destiny to God.

Journal Exercise

Write about the responsibilities of an immortal being. Why is it different being a soul, which will never die, than being soulless? Do you feel different about yourself when you think of eternity?

Meditation

Pray or meditate about your destiny. Ask for guidance.

6. Will This Draw Me Closer to the Spirit?

These exercises, like the ones in the preceding section, are useful not only in the annual summing-up of self but also in daily life. They can help you make essential judgments and decisions; the last meditation should be repeated daily or more often.

Visualizing

Visualize the kind of spiritual life you want to lead. How will your choices affect it? Think of all the consequences.

Journal Exercise

How do you see God?

Meditation

Pray or meditate about your spiritual life. Express your thanks, worship, and ask questions. Take time to listen quietly for answers as well.

INTERPRETING THE RESULTS

Interpretation is an intuitive process. You should prepare for it, as you've prepared for all the exercises, with relaxation techniques and rituals. You should also wait a week or so after completing the last of the exercises before you try to interpret. The process of interpretation is the same for all the exercises in the book; you may want to spend time interpreting each chapter's exercises in order to focus on one area at a time, and then slate a weekend for pulling it all together.

Ideally you should interpret the results while alone on a weekend retreat, somewhere quiet and away from home. At least take the phone off the hook and arrange to be alone at home.

If you are in a serious relationship--perhaps considering marriage or a lifetime commitment--you may want your partner to do these exercises as well. Then the weekend interpretive retreat can be done together. Sharing your feelings, metaphors, exercises, visions, and art work can be the basis for a fruitful discussion of how your lives will mesh and how they will be held separate. If you don't feel you can trust your partner with these innermost feelings, it's time to reexamine the relationship.

The first step is to read everything you've written. It may hurt. Rereading some of the memories, daydreams, and ambitions will cause you the same pain as rereading old diaries or the love letters you wrote that rainy spring ten years ago. As you read, jot down recurring themes and desires.

If the results repeatedly tell you that you are warm and social, that you have an eye for beauty, that you need to see immediate results, that praise and approval are important to you, you know that solitary and dry jobs are not for you. You'll never be happy as a long-distance truck driver or an economist. If you like trucks or economics nonetheless, you could be a dispatcher or mechanic or a teacher of economics. In any case, the stones (taking into consideration your other aptitudes) give the clearest idea of what fields are best.

An example of the process may be helpful. Rosemary came to me with a problem. She knew she wanted to grow and change, but she couldn't decide what job would best express herself. She had already made many of the other discoveries in finding her destiny: She had found a loving husband (having discovered that heterosexual marriage and family life were for her), she had found the proper place to live, she had found that she wanted children. All that remained was a decision on her career. After going through some of these exercises with her, I discovered the following pattern.

--She liked people.

--She had a great deal of patience.

--People had always come to her for advice.

--She had some medical training and was interested in health issues.

--She had an analytical mind.

--She was detached. She knew her own boundaries and did not overidentify with others.

--She had a strong urge to help others.

Combining practical, intellectual, and emotional factors, I advised her to get involved with counseling. But which kind? The crystal she had chosen was aventurine: a combination of body and soul. She would do best as a yoga instructor and counselor or as a massage therapist. She felt the latter best fit her needs and is now studying acupuncture.

But work is not the only or the most important part of your destiny; being yourself is. Gradually you'll begin to see patterns in the wishes, the metaphors, even the music, that express you. Then it's easy to see the ways that your personality can be expressed in your life--ways of molding your life to the pattern of your soul.

Angela came to me for a reading, which revealed that she was unhappy in her job and her life in general. However, the problem with work was only a symptom of a deeper lack of fulfillment in her life. She was strongly psychic and knew she should have been using her powers to help others. Instead she was terrified by them and tried desperately to repress them. As a child she had been punished for knowing too much, and she deeply feared further punishment. Yet repressing her psychic energies was a drain on her vitality, and the powers, since they were not consciously accepted or controlled, worked their way into her dreams and frightened her further.

Instead of repressing her abilities, she needed training in how to use them. Through six months of hard work, she cleared the original block, learned to harness her abilities, and began to change her life. Now she is an established, skillful, and compassionate psychic reader. She doesn't have nightmares. She has a sense of fulfillment, knowing she is achieving her destiny through using her innate talents. She has a more satisfying job as well--a change that came about naturally because of the change in her.

Angela's story illustrates the truth that unused abilities come back to haunt you. Through the above exercises you have discovered much more of who and what you are. You also should know what you want.

LIVING WELL

Fulfilling destiny and discovering karma focus on the individual's uniqueness. But living well is a mission that all of us share. The world and its beauties were not created as a distraction from the spiritual heights. You're supposed to enjoy things, feel emotions, become a whole person. You're supposed to live well; that's what living is for.

What does living well entail? It's easy to give details that fit me but may not fit you; to a certain extent it's a relative concept. It has almost nothing to do with money--except that if you worship money you're likely to miss many of the nonmonetary pleasures you were meant to enjoy. (Why? Because if you worship--or overvalue--money, you'll tend to downplay anything not bought with cash, credit, or traveller's checks. Because the love of money tends toward a kind of paranoia, you'll be so busy wondering if anyone's going to steal your "precious"--see Gollum in Tolkien's *Lord of the Rings*--that you can't actually enjoy your "precious" or anything else.)

Living well presupposes a reverential (or at least respectful) attitude toward the world and all created things. If you feel that way, you'll try to understand ecology and live in harmony with the Earth instead of in warfare with it. You'll be thankful for the riches of the world, from soft cotton woven into patterns to clean water dancing in a waterfall or artesian well, from sunsets and moonrise to the lightning leaping from cloud to cloud.

Living well can perhaps be understood best by looking at it on different levels. On the physical level, it entails a warm awareness and appreciation of the world, of the goodness of ordinary life, which can be achieved by acknowledging death.

If you were told you had six months to live, you would almost certainly change your life. You would do what you've put off doing; you would change your priorities; you would live with a holy intensity. Rain and sunlight, love and music would take on new and deeper meaning to you; money would probably mean less to you. You would eat plain bread with joy, sensing in every bite the death and resurrection of the grain; the tender sprouts thrusting through the Earth; the still, hot days of harvest; the baker's floury hands and the long slow rising of the yeast. Your newfound sense of process and purpose would teach you to rejoice and be glad in the bread, and your rejoicing would nourish you. And-- since you'd be paying much more attention to what you're eating--you'd probably stop eating tasteless, cottony white bread and build yourself up with something closer to Earth and to human hands and skills. You would live well.

The reason our lives are wasted (and therefore dull) is that we forget both that we must die and that we are immortal. Your actions matter: You have all eternity to enjoy--or suffer--the consequences of choices you make today. Your actions matter: You have only the present moment in which to choose, enjoy, act, forgive, because the only certain thing in life is that it will end. This concept, known as *carpe diem* (seize the day), is familiar to any English major; much of the West's great poetry has that theme. It was brilliantly illustrated in *The Dead Poets Society*, a movie featuring Robin Williams. Learn to live now, because you will be dead soon. Do what is right, because the consequences last forever.

"You cannot kill time without murdering eternity," said Thoreau. Killing time implies boredom and wastefulness--not living well.

Urgency, freshness, and passion are the ways in which we are supposed to live. Your choice of work, your relationships with other people, your willingness to learn and grow and change and forgive, your attitude toward the created Universe and toward the Creator--all are transformed by the realization that what you do matters. Every second matters. Are you *now* living with the intensity compelled by our few short years?

On the psychological level, living well means becoming a whole person: doing whatever is necessary to heal yourself and your relations with other people. All too often, we accept a diminished life, a life devoid of strong emotions. Because we fear pain, we guard ourselves-- and thus lock out joy. Though enjoyment seems to play a large part in this discussion, enjoyment is not the only factor in living well. Willingness to feel the full range of emotions is. True life--lived to its core--will include a lot of pain, anger, sadness, grief, restlessness, uncertainty, and a host of other forbidden emotions. What do you do with them?

You feel them and you go on. If you repress them, they'll demand expression in another way. Emotions are like a river--the water has to go somewhere. You cannot your emotions off without doing yourself damage. If you deny them, after a while you'll stop feeling them; but they'll hide in the psychological level, almost inaccessible, and haunt you in nightmares, in body-image problems, in depressions, in sick relationships. In one way or another those unacceptable feelings will push for expression. It's far better to feel them, know them, find the source, and go on.

Becoming a whole person also helps heal your relationships with other people. When you are whole, you do not exploit or oppress or abuse others because you see them as humans. When you're not fully human, no one else is, either. You begin to love your neighbor as yourself; because you can love yourself you can love your neighbor.

This takes us at last into the most important issue. What is living well on a spiritual level? It is loving God and your neighbor. This is the law and the prophets; these essentials lie at the core of all great religions.

The techniques, exercises, and ideas given here are designed to help you know yourself. Knowing the glories and intricacies of the human soul is one way to begin to perceive the Creator, who has left fingerprints on everything created. But go on from there. The subtlety and majesty and playfulness and goodness of God can be known only through a personal relationship. God rewards the questing spirit who seeks the Creator, who longs for Jesus, who desires the Inner Light of the Holy Ghost. Without the holy love of God, no life is well lived.

"Except the Lord build the house, they labor in vain that build it; except the Lord keep the city, the watchman waketh but in vain. It is vain for you to rise up early, to sit up late, to eat the bread of sorrows, for so he giveth his beloved sleep" (Psalm 127:1-3).

NOTE

1. I should enter a caveat here: I am by no means convinced of the truth of reincarnation. There is evidence for and against it. I do, however, believe in an afterlife, and that our actions and beliefs on Earth determine the nature of that afterlife. Most of all, I believe that you need a relationship with God--an ongoing, breathing, loving, honest dialogue. There are many ways to open yourself to God: ritual and spontaneous prayer, meditation, reading spiritual works, living well, manual labor, and a thousand other ways. Ideally, every moment, act, and thought should be part of that mystical closeness. This kind of personal relationship presupposes a personal God, not mere cosmic forces; the deity of Jesus, who died for our sins and was resurrected; and the constant and loving presence of the Holy Spirit--sometimes called the Inner Light-- who continually tries to draw us closer to God. This is what I believe and what my work is premised upon.

Table 10.1: Crystals and Their Meanings

The crystal set consists of rose quartz, red cullet, red jasper, carnelian, cat's eye (known sometimes as tiger's eye), brown agate, aventurine, green quartz, hematite, sodalite, chevron amethyst, amethyst, clear crystal, half-clear crystal, silent stone (snow quartz), Montana agate, smoky quartz, and onyx.

Rose Quartz

Physical: Friendship, intimacy, closeness.
Psychological: Harmony and affection; close family ties; the need for love and approval.
Spiritual: Surrender to God.
Shadow: Giving in, lack of self-assertion, going along with the crowd.

Red Cullet

Physical: Individualism, passion, and sexuality.
Psychological: Passion, creation, art. Independence and rebellion.
Spiritual: Spiritual transformation and renewal, the spirit of seeking.
Shadow: Jealousy, self-centeredness.

Red Jasper

Physical: Restlessness, change, curiosity.
Psychological: Spirit of seeking, self-examination, analysis.
Spiritual: The spirit of the quest, of the pilgrim.
Shadow: Change for its own sake--or the refusal to change and grow.

Carnelian

Physical: Warm and affectionate friendships, parties, and celebrations.
Psychological: Emotional ties based on knowledge of the other person, not on mystery and uncertainty. The need to understand and analyze relationships.
Spiritual: Reverence for life. The attitude that pleasure is of God and is

therefore holy. Mystical union with God and all creation.
Shadow: Manipulativeness, lack of self-respect, overindulgence, hiding behind a social group.

Cat's-Eye

Physical: Insight, shrewdness, vision.
Psychological: The gift of understanding others' problems. Often the mark of someone who is dedicated to helping others.
Spiritual: Willingness to forgive, understanding the flaws of yourself and others.
Shadow: Judgmental spirit, cattiness, gossip.

Brown Agate

Physical: Caution and good judgment. Slow and careful preparation.
Psychological: Self-discipline.
Spiritual: Penance, justice, scrupulous fairness.
Shadow: Pessimism, gloom, worry (often over petty matters). Insecurity and fear.

Green Quartz

Physical: Strength of character, self-esteem.
Psychological: Blending the unconscious with the conscious. Willingness to face your own dark side. The ability to interpret dreams.
Spiritual: The Kingdom of God within you.
Shadow: Nightmares, phobias, emotional problems. The separation of spiritual and physical life.

Aventurine

Physical: Great physical enjoyment, health, taking pleasure in the body.
Psychological: Balance between body, soul, and spirit. A healthy and innocent enjoyment of physical pleasures.
Spiritual: Freely offering of the body to God.
Shadow: Physical illness, stress, and separation from (or too much absorption in) the body.

Hematite

Physical: Enduring love, desire controlled by idealism, complete commitment.
Psychological: The discipline to transform dreams into reality. Sustained commitment to a dream.
Spiritual: Continuing devotion to God despite adverse circumstances.
Shadow: Rigidity, fault-finding. Inability to make a commitment or stick to a project.

Sodalite

Physical: Achievement, success, hard work rewarded.
Psychological: Getting your just desserts--knowing what you deserve and asking for it.
Spiritual: Freedom from greed, taking no thought for the morrow.
Shadow: Materialism, greed, lack of compassion.

Chevron Amethyst

Physical: Organization, structure, neatness.
Psychological: The final integration of the personality.
Spiritual: The order of heaven.
Shadow: Snobbishness, wrong priorities, inhuman bureaucracy.

Amethyst

Physical: Psychic talents combined with common sense. Great success.
Psychological: Psychic powers used well, self-knowledge and self-control.
Spiritual: A true spirit. Proper values.
Shadow: Using psychic knowledge for destructive purposes (very dangerous).

Crystal (clear)

Physical: Psychic abilities and clarity of outlook. Emotional harmony and peace.
Psychological: The integrated personality. Good relationships with oth-

ers based on self-respect.
Spiritual: Clear views of spiritual truth.
Shadow: Arrogance, fear of change.

Crystal (half-clear)

Physical: Confusion, hasty or prejudiced thinking. Not letting yourself
see the whole situation.
Psychological: Hiding the truth from yourself (usually to protect some-
one else).
Spiritual: The beginning of wisdom: knowing that you don't know.
Shadow: Refusing to trust yourself.

Silent Stone (white)

Physical: New beginnings and ideas.
Psychological: Waiting for the right time to make new beginnings.
Spiritual: The start of a new way of thinking. Protecting new ideas from
hostile people.
Shadow: Overly cautious or overly eager.

Montana Agate

Physical: Memories and persons from the past turn up. Opportunities to
correct past mistakes.
Psychological: Unconscious worries or influences from the past.
Spiritual: Remembering past problems in order to avoid them in the
future.
Shadow: Restraint, fear, lack of forgiveness of yourself and others.

Smoky Quartz

Physical: The ability or need to conceal yourself from other people. A
dramatic temperament.
Psychological: Hiding your true self in order to be liked or accepted.
Adaptability.
Spiritual: Struggling to find a true path. The faith is there, but the way is
not evident.
Shadow: Self-blame, hypersensitivity.

Onyx

Physical: Strength, courage, endurance.
Psychological: Getting to the root of the problem--a painful but necessary process.
Spiritual: Rebirth after a period of suffering and dryness.
Shadow: Giving up; refusing to enjoy anything for fear it will be taken away.

Further References

The books listed here are basic resources for discovering more about yourself and about the spiritual life. They are mostly nontechnical, self-help books. The list is by no means exhaustive; for example, it does not include the many reference works I have consulted or the highly technical astrology, tarot, and psychology books that are meant for those with advanced knowledge of the field. I have listed only those books that have a bearing on personal transformation through myth, divination, meditation, and so forth.

Bettelheim, Bruno. *The Uses of Enchantment.* New York: Vintage, 1975. The pioneering work on the meaning of fairy tales. Read it to discover your own fairy tale.

Bolen, Jean Shinoda. *Goddesses in Everywoman* and *Gods in Everyman.* New York: Harper and Row, Publishers Inc., 1984 and 1989. Two books that help you identify the god or goddess archetypes that influence you most strongly. Very highly recommended.

Bolles, Richard Nelson. *What Color Is Your Parachute?* Berkeley: Ten Speed Press, 1987. A marvelous series of exercises designed to help you find out what you want to do.

Campbell, Joseph, with Bill Moyers. *The Power of Myth.* New York: Doubleday, 1988. The perfect place to start on Campbell's vast vision of mythology. Also available as a set of videotapes. You may want to go on to his more exhaustive works, which are now, thanks to the PBS television show on which this book is based, available even in chain book-stores.

Faith and Practice. Philadelphia: Philadelphia Yearly Meeting, 1979. The use of queries--questions to ask yourself--is an old Quaker custom. Includes a list of queries that you may find helpful, as well as some meditations and readings.

Fields, Rick, *et. al. Chop Wood, Carry Water*. Los Angeles: Jeremy P. Tarcher, 1984. A guide to all aspects of spiritual fulfillment.

Gawain, Shakti. *Creative Visualization*. New York: Bantam, 1982. A brief but essential guide to the techniques and uses of visualizing.

Goldsmith, Joel S. *The Contemplative Life*. Secaucus, N.J.: Citadel Press, 1963. An extraordinary and lyrical handbook on meditation and living in the Spirit.

Greene, James, and David Lewis. *Know Your Own Mind*. New York: Rawson Associates, 1983. A series of tests to determine your skills in different areas.

Greene, Liz. *Relating*. York Beach, Maine: 1977. If you buy only one astrology book, this should be it. Greene is a Jungian psychologist and perhaps the finest astrologer alive.

Greer, Mary K. *Tarot for Your Self*. Van Nuys, Calif.: Newcastle, 1984. A tarot book that calls on both Eastern and Western mystic traditions to create new ways of self-discovery. The other two books of the cycle (*Tarot Constellations* and *Tarot Mirrors*) continue the good work.

Hillman, James. *The Dream and the Underworld*. New York: Harper and Row, Publishers Inc., 1979. A new psychology of dreams that will help you find the mythic content of your dreams.

Judith, Anodea. *Wheels of Life*. St. Paul, Minn.: Llewellyn, 1988. An important guide to the chakra system.

Kelynda, *The Crystal Tree*. West Chester, Pa.: Whitford, 1987. A new way of divination, using 18 crystals and colored stones on a Tree of Life board (stones and board included). Includes links with astrology, numerology, tarot, the four elements, the Kabbalah, and Western mysticism, as well as information on crystal use.

Leonard, Linda Schierse. *On the Way to the Wedding.* Boston: Shambhala, 1987. An extraordinary exploration of the psychological and spiritual meaning of the quest for a soulmate. Worth reading even if you have already found yours. Leonard's previous book, *The Wounded Woman,* examines the pain of the negative father/daughter relationship. Men should read it to understand how they can affect their daughters; women should read it to understand how their fathers affected them.

Lewis, C.S. *Surprised by Joy.* New York: Harcourt, Brace, Jovanovich, 1955. Lewis's autobiography is an excellent introduction to his thoughts. (If you prefer, you can read the *Chronicles of Narnia*--all seven volumes--and come to his work that way.) Read Lewis for his sense of the holiness and sweetness of ordinary life, the glorious order and pattern of the Universe. He's occasionally sexist, but with so many other spiritual treasures in his work, that can be forgiven. Once you've read this book, go on and read all his others.

Nichols, Sallie. *Jung and Tarot.* York Beach, Maine: Weiser, 1980. This exploration of the Jungian symbolism of the major arcana should not be missed for anyone interested in the deeper meaning of the Tarot.

Phillips, Dorothy Berkley; Elizabeth Boyden Howes; and Lucille M. Nixon. *The Choice Is Always Ours.* Wheaton, Ill.: Re-Quest Books, 1982. A series of brief readings in finding the Path. It brings together quotations from many and varied sources, some of them now difficult to find (the original version was published in 1948).

Progoff, Ira. *At a Journal Workshop.* New York: Dialogue House Library, 1975. The Intensive Journal (TM) technique for self-discovery. Progoff also gives workshops using this book as his basic text.

Rainer, Tristine. *The New Diary.* Los Angeles: Jeremy P. Tarcher, 1978. More on journal writing, less intense and more open than Progoff. Both books are very useful.

The Way of a Pilgrim and *The Pilgrim Continues His Way*, trans. by R.M. French. New York: Seabury Press, 1968. An anonymous classic--originally written in Russian--of the spiritual life.

About the Author

Kelynda has been a professional psychic since 1980, though she began to explore the realms of divination, myth, and symbol many years earlier. She is the creator of *The Crystal Tree* (Whitford Press, 1987), a new method of divination that combines the interpretation of crystals and colored gemstones with the Tree of Life, a symbol derived from the ancient traditions of the Kabbalah. The 200-page book is packaged with eighteen polished stones and a Tree of Life board. Other works include an essay in *Your Future Lives*, edited by Skye Alexander (Whitford Press, 1988).

In addition to her metaphysical writing, Kelynda does personal counseling with the Tarot, Star + Gate, and *The Crystal Tree*. Her astrological and numerological interpretation and counseling are available by mail; for a brochure, call (215) 284-3118 and leave a message or write to Kelynda, Box 201, Clifton Heights, PA 19018. She also teaches private classes for selected students and gives workshops, lectures, and seminars to groups.

Kelynda live in Pennsylvania with her husband, several cats, and (so far) about 3000 books. She spends her spare time helping her husband renovate their Victorian house.

More exciting titles from Whitford Press

Origin and Destiny of Humanity William Earl Valentine Key-nee. "In order to truly understand why we all are here on Planet Earth as well as our place in the universe, we must embark on an unprecedented journey. This voyage will take us through various fields of study with a multi-disciplinary approach. The end result will demonstrate how interconnected we are with the universe itself."

In *Origin and Destiny of Humanity*, William Key-nee explores our physical, intellectual, and spiritual connections with the universe. In six chapters Mr. Key-nee discusses our development from the first man and woman to the people of the future; the physical development of Earth; the life mastery achieved by the avatars (Pythagoras, Confucius, Christ, and others); the New Age movement and its future goals; social, human, and scientific cycles; UFOs; and other fascinating and informative topics. *Origin and Destiny of Humanity* provides a brief survey of humanity's progress and an optimistic view of humanity's future as we embrace the advances and changes in technology, religion, science, and mind science. By challenging our traditional beliefs and broadening our perspectives, Mr. Key-nee believes we can greatly enhance our quality of life and peacefully move into the twenty-first century. This work is a compelling study that helps the reader "better grapple with the awesome revolution in thought that we are undergoing at this time in the still very young history of Planet Earth."

Origin and Destiny of Humanity is captivating reading for anyone, and especially will intrigue those with a budding or deep interest in the New Age movement.

Size: 6 1/4" x 9 1/4"   paperbound   160 pp.
ISBN: 0-924608-00-5 $9.95

Planets in Synastry: Astrological Patterns of Relationships E.W. Neville. At its simplest level, synastry is the examination of the interaction of two astrological charts. Since questions about the relationship are perhaps the ones most often asked of the astrologer, the art of synastry is a basic skill to practice astrology at any but the most casual level.

Planets in Synastry takes the reader through the steps of this complex process. Individual phases of a relationship are set out and a method for analysis of each phase is described. It focuses not only on the analysis of synastry, but on the translation of the insights into real life applications.

This is an important addition to the Whitford *Planets* series by one of America's foremost authorities. *Planets in Synastry* will be a welcome addition to every astrological library.

Size: 6 1/4" x 9 1/4"   paperbound   276 pp.
ISBN: 0-924608-01-3 $14.95

The Crystal Tree Kelynda. This fascinating and original method of divination combines the mystery of the Kabbalistic Tree of Life and the magic of gemstones. Find answers to perplexing questions and gain insight into yourself. This extraordinary book comes complete with eighteen different gemstones and a full-color board to use in your readings. (Whitford)

Size: 6 1/8" x 9 1/4"   full-color board   192 pp.
ISBN: 0-914918-73-7   paperbound $24.95

An Act of Woman Power Kisma K. Stepanich. An invaluable book for every man and woman who is ready to understand the origin of their essence; to go beyond the threshold of self-imposed limitations and begin working on a true and balanced level of attunement with our potential power.

An Act of Woman Power is an example of one woman's journey into the very center of this power. It goes beyond the normal "how-to" or "self-help" books because the ultimate outcome of the step-by-step guidance is an awakening of all the senses, the rising of potential energy, and a deep merging and connection with our greatest support system: Mother Earth. (Whitford)

Size: 6 1/4" x 9 1 4"   paperbound   160 pp.
ISBN: 0-914918-93-1 $9.95

Expand Your Psychic Skills Enid Hoffman. In this sequel to her best-selling *Develop Your Psychic Skills*, Hoffman shows you how to use your innate psychic abilities to improve your daily life. Dozens of techniques, exercises, games and meditations are included to help you fully utilize your inner resources. (Whitford)

Size: 6 1/2" x 9 1/4"   paperbound   144 pp.
ISBN: 0-914918-72-9 $9.95

Exploring the Power Within: A Resource Book for Transcending the Ordinary Brad Steiger. Brad Steiger shares insights from more than 30 present-day spiritual leaders who have demonstrated remarkable powers of mind, body, and spirit. Through fascinating life histories and personal interviews, Steiger invites us to learn from such notables as Irene Hughes, Olof Jonnson, Jane Roberts, John Catchings, Olga Worrall, Deon Frey, and many others. (Whitford)

Size: 6 1/4" x 9 1/4"   paperbound   280 pp.
ISBN: 0-914918-97-4 $14.95

A Look at Tomorrow Today Leonard Cataldo and Robert Pelletier. In this compelling and fascinating study, authors Cataldo and Pelletier invite the reader to find and utilize the vast riches within. The reader will discover that not only is he a constituent of one of the twelve zodiacal signs, but also what that means and how it influences his life and behavior.

A Look at Tomorrow Today is a valuable resource for novice and experienced astrologers and those with an interest in astrology.

Size: 6 1/4" x 9 1/4" paperbound 500 pp.
ISBN: 0-914918-94-X $18.95

Develop Your Psychic Skills Enid Hoffman. This bestseller shows that we all have psychic abilities waiting to be developed. Includes exercises for training both perceptive and projective skills, for clearing obstructive beliefs, for past-life recall, and more. (Whitford)

Size: 6 1/2" x 9 1/4" paperbound 192 pp.
ISBN: 0-914918-29-X $9.95

Indian Medicine Power Brad Steiger. *Indian Medicine Power* provides each reader with a path from yesterday to tomorrow that allows for individual growth, awareness, and an accessibility to the ancient mysteries that continue to be practiced today. (Whitford)

Size: 6 1/2" x 9 1/4" paperbound 216 pp.
ISBN: 0-914918-65-6 $12.95

Keys for Self-Realization: A Self-Counseling Manual Marilyn Jean Enners. In the search for Enlightenment and Knowledge there are many different "keys" available to the seeker which unlock the gate to the Subconscious Mind, the channel to the Higher Self. In this book Marilyn Jean Enners examines these keys and how they may be used by the person seeking self-realization.

Among these keys are Meditation, Tarot, Astrology, Numerology, Color Symbolism, and Dream Analysis. By integrating these various metaphysical sciences she enables the readers to see the possibilities that exist for them. (Whitford)

Size: 6" x 9" paperbound 320 pp.
ISBN: 0-914918-91-5 $17.95

Numerology, Astrology, and Dreams Dusty Bunker. Well-known numerologist, dream researcher, and astrologer Dusty Bunker shows you how to interpret your dreams as they relate to important and predictable life cycles. She reveals the meanings of numbers and symbols in dreams and examines the types of dreams people of each astrological sign are likely to have. (Whitford)

Size: 6 1/4" x 9 1/4" paperbound 198 pp.
ISBN: 0-914918-74-5 $13.95

Your Future Lives Enid Hoffman, Brad Steiger, et al. Much has been written about the significance of past lives, but perhaps where we're going is more important than where we've been. This unique anthology shows you how to work through problem areas in your current lifetime so that your future lives will be happier and healthier. Each of the seven contributing authors, including Brad Steiger, Enid Hoffman and others, approach the challenge from a different perspective, and offer techniques, exercises, meditations, and games to help you get started. A great investment in your future. (Whitford)

Size: 6 1/4" x 9 1/4" paperbound 160 pp.
ISBN: 0-914918-82-6 $12.95